——— MIND MATTERS ———

Do We Have Free Will?

—— MIND MATTERS ——

Series editor: Judith Hughes

In the same series

———— MIND MATTERS ————

do we have free will?

MARK THORNTON

PUBLISHED BY ST. MARTIN'S PRESS

All rights reserved. For information, write:
Scholarly and Reference Division,
St. Martin's Press, Inc., 175 Fifth Avenue, New York, NY 10010

First published in the United States of America in 1989

Printed in Great Britain

ISBN 0-312-03146-7

Library of Congress Cataloging-in-Publication Data

Thornton, Mark.
      Do we have free will? / Mark Thornton.
        p. cm. – (Mind matters)
      Bibliography: p.
      Includes Index.
      ISBN 0-312-03146-7
      1. Free will and determinism. I. Title. II. Series.
      BJ1461.T38 1989
      123'.5 – dc 19   89-30335
                                                        CIP

contents

foreword

'A philosophical problem has the form *I don't know my way about*,' said Wittgenstein. These problems are not the ones where we need information, but those where we are lost for lack of adequate signposts and landmarks. Finding our way – making sense out of the current confusions and becoming able to map things both for ourselves and for others – is doing successful philosophy. This is not quite what the lady meant who told me when I was seven that I ought to have more philosophy, because philosophy was eating up your cabbage and not making a fuss about it. But that lady *was* right to suggest that there were some useful skills here.

Philosophizing, then, is not just a form of highbrow chess for postgraduate students; it is becoming conscious of the shape of our lives, and anybody may need to do it. Our culture contains an ancient tradition which is rich in helpful ways of doing so, and in Europe they study that tradition at school. Here, that study is at present being squeezed out even from university courses. But that cannot stop us doing it if we want to. This series contains excellent guide-books for people who do want to, guide-books which are clear, but which are not superficial surveys. They are themselves pieces of real philosophy, directed at specific problems which are likely to concern all of us. Read them.

MARY MIDGLEY

preface

Philosophers are very good at talking to one another. Some of them are also good at talking with other people. In the market-places of Athens, the cafés of Paris, and lately, in the pubs of London, philosophers have always found a public bursting with its own ideas and keen to discuss them with others. The need to ask and attempt to answer philosophical questions is in us all and is prompted sometimes by particular events in our personal lives and sometimes by a more general unease about wider social or political or scientific issues. At such times there is always a popular demand for philosophers to explain themselves and the views of their illustrious forebears in ways which others can understand and question and use.

It is not an easy thing to do because Philosophy is not easy, though its central insights, like those in the sciences, are often startlingly simple. To gain those insights we all have to follow the paths of reasoning for ourselves. Signposts have been left for us by the great philosophers of the past, and deciphering some of them is part of the business of this series.

'Mind Matters' is not 'Philosophy Made Easy' but rather 'Philosophy Made Intelligible', and the authors in this series have been chosen for more than their philosophical knowledge. Some of them are also experts in other fields such as medicine, computing or biology. All are people who recognise and try to practise the art of writing in an accessible and clear manner, believing that philosophical thought which is not understandable is best kept to oneself. Many have acquired this ability in the harsh discipline of adult education where students bring their own knowledge and puzzles to the subject and demand real explanations of relevant issues.

Each book in this series begins with a perplexing question that we may ask ourselves without, perhaps, realising that we are 'philosophising': Do computers have minds? Can a pile of bricks be a work of art? Should we hold pathological killers responsible for their crimes? Such questions are considered and new questions raised with frequent reference to the views of major philosophers. The authors go further than this, however. It is not their intention to produce a potted history of philosophical ideas. They also make their own contributions to the subject, suggesting different avenues of thought to explore. The result is a collection of original writings on a wide range of topics produced for all those who find Philosophy as fascinating and compelling as they do.

'Do We Have Free Will?' is not just an abstract philosophical question, because our answer to it has enormous influence in many areas of our lives. It shapes educational and legal theory, it underlies particular views in Sociology and Psychology, and it is apparent in decisions in social and political policy.

Mark Thornton has produced an elegant and comprehensive guide to the rich variety of philosophical opinion on the subject. His clear exposition, penetrating criticism and original suggestions make this a valuable book for anyone with a practical or a theoretical concern with issues of human freedom and responsibility.

JUDITH HUGHES

1: what is the question and why does it matter?

People have debated the question of free will for centuries because it is so central to our self-understanding. Is it just human vanity to think that we are different from other things because we have free will? Or is free will an essential part of human nature?

To answer the question 'Do we have free will?' we need an answer to the question 'What is free will?' Unfortunately this is not a simple question. We shall have to look at both questions together and we shall not have an answer to either question until we reach the end of our inquiry. I assume you and I are both interested in the question of free will, hence you and I both have some idea of what it is that we're interested in. Without trying to be too precise at this point, let us consider the important features of free will.

First, someone with free will is *autonomous* in the sense that he or she has a 'will' of his or her own: she wants certain things and makes her own decisions, without being pushed into them by outside pressures and forces. Second, someone with free will has genuine *alternatives* open to him or her, as in Hamlet's 'To be or not to be'. If we have free will then we do not *have* to decide one way rather than another; we can decide on whichever we want. *Autonomy* and *alternatives* come together in the idea *choice*. In choosing we make our own contribution to the future by selecting one course of action from among alternatives.

But do we have autonomy and are there genuine alternatives open to us? Autonomy seems to vanish once we consider all the influences making us what we are. Are we in the grip of our heredity and environment? And although there may *in theory* seem to be alternatives open to us, *in practice* and especially with hindsight there looks to be a tiresome inevitability about our choices. As a character in B.F. Skinner's *Walden Two* puts it, 'Linguistically or logically there seem to be two possibilities, but I submit that there's only one in fact.'

Reformers like Skinner believe that overthrowing the 'myth' of free will will lead to far-reaching and beneficial changes in our social practices. For instance, he believes that the institutions of criminal justice and punishment presuppose that people have free will. Once we abandon the idea of free will, we can give up blaming and punishing people and instead practise a system of 'positive reinforcement', which, he believes, is far more effective in getting people to behave in socially approved ways. The character Frazier in *Walden Two* represents Skinner; Castle is his 'old-fashioned' opponent:

> "Now," Frazier continued earnestly, "if it's in our power to create any of the situations which a person likes or to remove any situation he doesn't like, we can control his behaviour. When he behaves as we want him to behave, we simply create a situation he likes, or remove one he doesn't like. As a result, the probability that he will behave that way again goes up, which is what we want. Technically it's called 'positive re-inforcement'.
>
> "The old school made the amazing mistake of supposing that the reverse was true, that by removing a situation a person likes or setting up one he doesn't like – in other words by punishing him – it was possible to *reduce* the probability that he would behave in a given way again. That simply doesn't hold. It has been established beyond question...
>
> "Now that we *know* how positive reinforcement works and why negative doesn't," he said at last, "we can be more de-liberate, and hence more successful in our cultural design. We can achieve a sort of control under which the controlled, though they are following a code much more scrupulously than was ever the case under the old system, nevertheless *feel free*. ..
>
> "No, Mr. Castle, when a science of behaviour has once been achieved, there's no alternative to a planned society. We can't

leave mankind to an accidental or biased control. But by using the principle of positive reinforcement – carefully avoiding force or the threat of force – we can preserve a personal sense of freedom."

Whatever one may think of Skinner's *Walden Two* he is clearly right to believe that our social institutions do presuppose a certain view of human beings. If we want *good* social institutions, then, we had better form a *correct* idea of ourselves.

As we shall see, three different approaches dominate the current debate. According to one, represented by Skinner, psychology has shown convincingly that we do not have free will, or at least has made it 'more and more plausible'. The idea of free will is simply obsolete from a scientific point of view.

According to the second, psychology can never be a complete science of human nature. There are aspects of ourselves for ever beyond the scientific purview. Just because scientific psychology is successful in some areas that doesn't mean it will be successful in all. In fact it is only successful in the simpler, more predictable, more mechanical and habitual spheres of human behaviour, precisely those areas where free will does not manifest itself. Free will may be an aspect of ourselves that the scientific psychologist cannot turn into science. The scientist is *not* entitled to say 'Free will doesn't exist': since scientists are only in a position to make assertions about what lies *within* science; they are not in a position to say that what lies *outside* their science doesn't exist.

According to the third approach, the first two views make the same mistake: the mistake of thinking that the more we know about the causes of human behaviour, the less do we believe that humans have free will – so that if we had a complete scientific account of human psychology, that would prove that human beings do not have free will at all. (The disagreement between the two views is about whether there can be a complete scientific psychology.) The third view says that a complete scientific psychology, though unlikely in fact because of the complexity of our thought processes and behaviour, would not show that we do not have free will. Rather, it would provide a complete scientific explanation of how it is that we have free will. It would explain our free will, it would not explain it away. Our free will would be left intact.

Suppose that we do have free will. Is this something desirable, something we should be glad of? Sartre suggests that 'it is in *anguish* that man gets the consciousness of his freedom'. He depicts a gambler who has resolved to give up gambling but 'who when he approaches the gambling table, suddenly sees all his resolutions melt away'; 'what he apprehends then in anguish is precisely the total inefficacy of the past resolution':

> It seemed to me that I had established a *real barrier* between gambling and myself...After having patiently built up barriers and walls, after enclosing myself in the magic circle of a resolve, I perceive with anguish that *nothing* prevents me from gambling.

This perception that nothing prevents him is the consciousness of freedom.

Wouldn't it be better if we were conditioned to do what is good for us? Is free will perhaps the enemy of happiness? People who want to give up smoking sometimes go to hypnotists who will 'make them' give up smoking after they have 'tried' to give it up but can't do it 'of their own free will'. But what if someone didn't want to go to a hypnotist 'of his own free will', although he knows that he would be happier if he did do because he really does want to give up smoking? Perhaps he should be hypnotised into wanting to go to a hypnotist! He would be happier and he would get what he wanted.

The tension between happiness and freedom is at the centre of Aldous Huxley's *Brave New World*:

> "Don't you wish you were free, Lenina?"
> "I don't know what you mean. I am free. Free to have the most wonderful time. Everybody's happy nowadays."
> He laughed, "Yes, 'Everybody's happy nowadays.' We begin giving the children that at five. But wouldn't you like to be free to be happy in some other way, Lenina? In your own way, for example; not in everybody else's way."
> "I don't know what you mean," she repeated. Then, turning to him, "Oh, do let's go back, Bernard," she besought; "I do so hate it here."

Bernard felt enslaved by his conditioning; but that only shows it hadn't worked.

Those who would rather be happy than free tend not to believe in free will. Those who think free will is the distinguishing mark of human dignity tend to believe in it. Those who think free will is just an excuse for inhumane treatment of criminals and the poor tend not to believe in free will. Those who think that the denial of free will is part of a dastardly plot to undermine the traditions of Western society tend to believe in it. Those who think that the idea of free will is an obstacle to scientific progress tend not to believe in free will, except that those who regard free will as a welcome obstacle to so-called scientific 'progress' tend to favour free will. Free will, according to some, is an idea whose time has gone. Has it?

notes

B.F. Skinner. 20th century American psychologist. Author of *Walden Two,* a fictional account of a society based on Skinner's behavioural techniques, and *Beyond Freedom and Dignity*, as well as other books on behavioural psychology. Quotations are from ch. 29 of *Walden Two*.

Jean-Paul Sartre. 20th century French philosopher and writer. Author of *Being and Nothingness*, in which Sartre expounds his philosophy of existentialism, and of many novels and plays. Quotations are from *Being and Nothingness* Pt. 1, ch. 1, sec. V. Sartre's views on freedom are discussed further in ch. 2.

Aldous Huxley. 20th century English novelist. Quotations are from *Brave New World*, ch. 6.

2: historical overview

Various strands run through the history of our topic. One is the attempt to understand human nature: is it special? and if so in what way? Another is religious: if God created us and knows exactly what we are going to do, is there any room for free will? A third is scientific: if science can explain everything we do, does that mean that free will is an illusion? Different issues predominate at different times: in Greek philosophy, the first; in medieval philosophy, the second; in 17th and 18th century philosophy, the third. In 20th century philosophy, with the rise of the science of psychology, the first and third issues predominate.

Greek philosophy (5th/4th centuries B.C.)
The Greeks did not have a word that means exactly what our term 'free will' means. But they did have a word, usually translated as 'voluntary', which played much the same role in their thought as 'free will' does in ours. Although the Greek philosophers, notably Socrates, Plato and Aristotle, were not directly concerned with the religious and scientific questions which troubled later thinkers, they do have some interesting views which are relevant to what we would call free will.

Socrates wrote nothing, but is known to us through the writings of others, particularly Plato. Socrates held that everyone naturally seeks after what is good; but of course not everyone does what *is* good. His explanation was that we are *ignorant* or *deceived* about what is good. Voluntary action, i.e. action aimed at what is good, thus becomes contrasted with acts done through ignorance:

> No man voluntarily pursues evil, or that which he thinks to be evil. To pursue what one believes to be evil rather than what is good is not in human nature; and when a man is compelled to choose one of two evils, no one will choose the greater when he may have the less.

For Socrates *virtue is knowledge:* to know what is good is to seek to achieve it. Nothing more is required since everyone desires what is good.

Plato agrees with Socrates that to act voluntarily is to follow reason and pursue what is good. But he denies that knowledge of what is good is all that is necessary. Plato depicts the 'soul' (*psyche*) as divided into three 'parts' or aspects: Reason, Spirit (emotion) and Appetite (desire). Although Reason may know what is good, it may be overpowered by Appetite. In that case a person does not act from her free will, but under compulsion. The proper condition of a person's soul is when he or she acts according to Reason; but sometimes Appetite seeks to dominate or Spirit is no longer ruled by Reason:

> Reason ought to rule, having the ability and foresight to act for the whole, and Spirit ought to obey and support it...When these two elements have been brought up and trained to their proper function, they must be put in charge of Appetite, which forms the greater part of each person's make-up and is naturally insatiable. They must prevent it taking its fill of the so-called physical pleasures, for otherwise it will get too large and strong and will try to subject and control the other elements, which it has no right to do, and so wreck life entirely.

Plato's view is very closely echoed by Plotinus (in the 3rd century A.D.):

> When our Soul holds to its Reason-Principle, to the guide, pure and detached and native to itself, only then can we speak of personal operation, of voluntary act. Things so done may truly be described as *our* doing, for they have no other source; they are the issue of the unmingled Soul, a Principle that is a First, a leader, a sovereign not subject to the errors of ignorance, not to be overthrown by the tyranny of the desires which, where they can break in, drive and drag us, so as to allow of no act of *ours* but mere response to stimulus.

Sometimes Appetite seeks to dominate or Spirit is no longer ruled by Reason.

This clearly connects the ideas of an act being voluntary, being *our* doing, and proceeding from reason.

Aristotle defines a voluntary act as 'one of which the moving principle is in the agent himself, he being aware of the particular circumstances of the action'. He contrasts voluntary acts, as Socrates did, with acts done through ignorance and also, as Plato did, with acts done from compulsion: 'Those things, then, are considered involuntary which take place under compulsion or owing to ignorance.'

Aristotle holds as a general principle that 'where it is in our power to act it is also in our power not to act and *vice versa*'. But he realizes that this principle cannot be taken for granted. Those who deny that we have free will would reject this principle: perhaps those who fail to do what they ought *cannot* do what they ought. Aristotle takes a hard line:

> Still they are themselves by their slack lives responsible for becoming people of that kind; and people are themselves responsible for being wrongdoers or profligates when they spend their time cheating people or in drinking and such activities. They acquire a particular character by acting in a particular manner.

Just as someone can voluntarily make herself ill through living in a way she knows will make her ill, so someone can voluntarily make herself wicked:

> the unjust and the profligate might at the beginning have avoided becoming so; and therefore they are so voluntarily, even if now that they have become so it is not possible for them not to be so.

If it was once in a man's power not to be wicked, then in being wicked he is so voluntarily.

But is this correct? Suppose someone through no fault of his own believes that it is all right to lead an immoral life. Surely it is not his fault that vice appears good to him? Aristotle replies that 'if this theory is correct, how will virtue be voluntary any more than vice?' Of course some would accept this conclusion and would agree that the virtuous cannot be praised any more than the wicked can be blamed. But there is a long tradition in Western thought, going back to Socrates and extending to the present, according to which vice is less voluntary than virtue.

There are important disagreements between Socrates, Plato and Aristotle. But they all emphasize the fact that we are rational beings, that is to say, rational as opposed to non-rational, not to irrational. We are capable of judging things to be good or bad and acting in the light of that knowledge.

medieval philosophy

In the 13th century A.D. St. Thomas Aquinas presented, in his massive work the *Summa Theologiae,* a synthesis of Aristotelian and Christian thought, which became the official philosophy of the Roman Catholic Church. Earlier Christian philosophers, e.g. St. Augustine, had been most influenced by Plato; but Aquinas was far more influenced by Aristotle.

Aquinas held that human beings have free will. God certainly knows everything we will do, since he is omniscient. But, in Aquinas' view, it does not follow that we do not act freely. What he knows is that we *freely* choose to do this, or that. Again, God has created us, and since God is omnipotent and can do anything which is conceivable, he can certainly create free beings. Aquinas argues for free will in this way:

> Human beings have free will. Otherwise counsels, precepts, prohibitions, rewards and punishments would be pointless.
>
> In order to make this evident, we must consider that some things act without judgement; as a stone falls downward; and all things which lack knowledge are like this. And some act from judgement, but not a free judgement; thus brute animals. For a sheep, seeing a wolf, thinks that it ought to run away, from a natural and not a free judgement; it does it by natural instinct and not by thinking about it. And this holds true of any judgement made by brute animals. But human beings act from judgement because through their cognitive powers they decide that something is to be avoided or sought after. But because this judgement in a particular case does not come from a natural instinct but from rational comparison of alternatives, human beings act freely and can be inclined towards opposite decisions...And so in regard to particular acts reason's judgement is open to various possibilities, not restricted to one. It is because human beings are rational that their will is necessarily free.

Aquinas also says:

> Choice is the distinguishing mark of free will. For we are said to be free in a decision when we can adopt one course of action and reject another; and this is to make a choice.

Thus Aquinas clearly locates our free will in our powers of reason and choice.

17th and 18th century philosophy

The modern problem of free will comes to the fore in the 17th century with the rise of science. Thanks to the work of Galileo, Newton and others, the physical world more and more seemed to be governed by universal laws of nature which do not allow any exceptions.

Galileo confirmed Copernicus' theories of our solar system and discovered the law of uniform acceleration of moving bodies in the early 17th century. Harvey discovered the circulation of the blood in 1628, an important discovery because it suggested that a living body is a mechanism like a clock. Boyle's law ('At a constant temperature the volume of a gas is inversely proportional to the pressure') was published in 1661. And the crowning touch, the law of gravity ('Every particle of matter in the universe attracts every other particle with a force that is proportional to the product of their masses and inversely proportional to the square of the distance between their centres') was discovered by Newton in 1687.

Now, if *everything* is governed by scientific laws and if, consequently, it is *necessary* that we act as we do, how can we be free in the sense of being able either to act or not to act as we choose? Aristotle and Aquinas had both contrasted freedom with necessity. Science seemed in the 17th century to be declaring itself in favour of necessity.

The most radical response to this threat to our freedom was Descartes'. Descartes held that the physical world is indeed governed by rigid scientific laws, but *our minds are not*. Our bodies are complicated physical mechanisms; but our minds, comprising all our powers of consciousness, reason and will, are not physical at all, and therefore they are exempt from physical laws. Mind can interact with body, according to Descartes; that is to say mental events can cause physical events and *vice versa*: for instance, bodily injuries can cause sensations of pain and we can move our limbs because we choose to do so. But the mental is not physical and therefore not governed by physical laws. The upshot is that we have complete freedom of will:

It is only will, or freedom of choice, that I experience in myself to such a degree that I cannot conceive of any greater; so that it is in this respect above all, I think, that I bear the likeness and image of God. For although God's will is incomparably greater than mine, both by reason of the knowledge and power which accompany it and make it firmer and more efficacious, and by reason of its object – of its greater scope –, yet it does not seem to be greater when considered precisely just as will. Will consists simply in the fact that we are able alike to do and not to do a given thing (that is, we can either assert or deny, either seek or shun); or rather, simply in the fact that our impulse toward what our intellects present to us as worthy of assertion or denial, or as a thing to be sought or shunned, is such that we feel ourselves not to be determined by any external force. There is no need for me to be impelled both ways in order to be free; on the contrary, the more I am inclined one way – either because I clearly understand it under the aspect of truth and goodness, or because God has so disposed my inmost consciousness – the more freely do I choose that way.

God, of course, is not governed by physical laws; neither, according to Descartes, are our minds.

Discussions of Descartes' view have usually focussed on his view of mind and body, which is generally referred to as 'Cartesian dualism'. Some have argued that if mind and body are as distinct as Descartes says they are, how can they interact? And if they do not then mind would be literally powerless so far as changes in the world are concerned: a free will which can be employed only within our own minds seems small comfort. Others have argued that the physical world as seen by science is a 'closed' system; that is to say, all physical changes have physical causes. In that case, too, mind, if it is not physical, will make no difference to what happens.

Spinoza held that Descartes' error was to think that because our *ideas* of mind and body are different, therefore mind and body themselves must actually be different. But in fact, according to Spinoza, 'the mind and the body are *one and the same thing*, conceived at one time under the attribute of thought, and at another time under that of extension.' That is, when we think of ourselves as Minds we are thinking of ourselves as thinking beings; when we think of ourselves as Bodies we are thinking of ourselves as being extended in space. But we are actually thinking of the *same thing*, only in different ways. Now, if mind and body are the same thing, then, corresponding to the scientific laws which govern the body and other physical objects, there must also be laws which govern the mind. Thus, in Spinoza's view, Descartes' dream of a world of mind exempt from rigid laws is just a dream: 'those who believe that they speak, or are silent, or do anything else from a free decree of the mind, dream with their eyes open.' Spinoza realizes, though, that the belief in freedom is hard to shake:

> Thus an infant believes that of its own free will it desires milk, an angry child believes that it freely desires vengeance, a timid child believes that it freely desires to run away...Experience, no less than reason, teaches us clearly that men believe themselves to be free simply because they are conscious of their actions and unconscious of the causes whereby those actions are determined; and, further, it is plain that the dictates of the mind are but another name for the appetites, and therefore vary according to the varying state of the body...All these considerations clearly show that a mental decision and a bodily appetite, or physically determined state, are simultaneous, or rather they are one and the same thing, which we call decision when it is considered and explained under the attribute of thought, and which we call a causally determined state when it is considered under the attribute of extension and deduced from the laws of motion and rest.

The belief that our minds are exempt from causal determination is thus dismissed as a product of our ignorance of the laws governing our physical and mental operations:

> What the body can do no one has hitherto determined, that is to say, experience has not yet taught anyone what the body by itself, without being determined by the mind, can and cannot do solely by the laws of nature, in so far as nature is considered merely as physical.

(More than three hundred years later we still don't know exactly how the brain works.)

Although Spinoza believed that freedom in Descartes' sense is an illusion, he did believe in freedom in another sense. In his discussion 'Of the Power of Understanding, or of Human

Freedom' he argues that human beings by the power of their reason can come to understand their emotions and thus gain freedom, though not complete control:

> At length I pass to the remaining portion of my Ethics, which is concerned with the way leading to freedom. I shall therefore examine therein the power of reason, showing how far reason may control the emotions, and what is the nature of Mental Freedom or Happiness. We shall then be able to see how much more powerful the wise man is than the ignorant.

We do not have absolute power over our emotions (that would only be possible if Descartes were right), but we have some power: 'no remedy within our power can be conceived which is more excellent for controlling our emotions than that which consists in a true knowledge of them.'

In the 17th century we find a view of free will coming to the fore which does not assert free will against necessity in the style of Descartes or necessity against free will in the style of Spinoza. Rather, it is argued that there is no fundamental opposition between free will and necessity. This argument is put forward forcefully by Thomas Hobbes in opposition to Dr. Bramhall, who was Bishop of Derry. Hobbes writes:

> It may be he thinks it all one to say, 'I was free to write it', and 'it was not necessary that I should write it'. But I think otherwise; for he is free to do a thing, that may do it if he have the will to do it, and may forbear if he have the will to forbear. And yet if there be a necessity that he shall have the will to do it, the action is necessarily to follow; and if there be a necessity that he shall have the will to forbear, the forbearing also will be necessary.

Bramhall replies equally forcefully:

> Judge then what a pretty kind of liberty it is which is maintained by T. H., such a liberty as is in little children before they have the use of reason, before they can consult or deliberate of anything. Is not this a childish liberty; and such a liberty as is in brute beasts, as bees and spiders, which do not learn their faculties as we do our trades, by experience and consideration? This is a brutish liberty...
>   Certainly all the freedom of the agent is from the freedom of the will...If it be precisely and inevitably determined in all

> occurrences whatsoever, what a man shall will, and what he shall not will, what he shall write, and what he shall not write, to what purpose is this power?...Either the agent is determined before he acts, what he shall will, and what he shall not will, what he shall act, and what he shall not act, and then he is no more free to act than he is to will; or else he is not determined, and then there is no necessity...If the will be determined, the writing or not writing is likewise determined, and then he should not say, 'he may write or he may forbear', but he must write or he must forbear.

But in Hobbes' view, to say 'he may write or he may forbear' is to say 'whether he writes or forbears depends on his will'; and this can be true even if his will is necessitated and determined. Hobbes believes that the question whether a person is *free* to will whatever she wills is an absurd one:

> I acknowledge this liberty, that I can do if I will; but to say, I can will if I will, I take to be an absurd speech.

My freedom consists in my being 'free to do if I will' not in my being 'free to will'. Hobbes believes that if Bramhall had had the wits to appreciate this distinction he would have realized that we are free although our wills are necessitated and determined.

Later in the 17th century John Locke presented a view of freedom which echoes Hobbes'. According to Locke, freedom 'consists in our being able to act, or not to act, according as we shall choose or will'. Locke, however, uses the term 'necessity' in a different way from Hobbes. For Locke freedom *is* opposed to necessity. Necessity, for Locke, means that something takes place *independently of our wills*. When we are subject to necessity we are in the same situation as an inanimate object:

> A tennis-ball, whether in motion by the stroke of a racket, or lying still at rest, is not by anyone taken to be a free agent. If we inquire into the reason, we shall find it is, because we conceive not a tennis-ball to think, and consequently not to have any volition, or preference of motion to rest, or vice versa; and therefore has not liberty, is not a free agent; but all its both motion and rest come under our idea of necessary, and are so called. Likewise a man falling into the water (a bridge breaking beneath him) has not herein liberty, is not a free agent. For

> though he has volition, though he prefers his not falling to his falling; yet the forbearance of that motion not being in his power; the stop or cessation of that motion follows not upon his volition; and therefore therein he is not free.

Thus in Locke's sense of 'necessary' the actions we choose and perform of our own volition are free, not necessary.

Like Hobbes, Locke locates freedom in the power to do what one wills, not in the will itself being free. In fact Locke hopes to 'put an end to that long-agitated, and I think unreasonable, because unintelligible question, viz., Whether man's will be free or no?' by insisting that 'liberty, which is but a power, belongs only to agents, and cannot be an attribute or modification of the will'. But many commentators are unconvinced. For instance Leibniz in a discussion of Locke's views wrote:

> When we reason about the liberty of the will, or about the free will, we do not ask if the man can do what he wills, but if there is enough independence in his will itself. We do not ask if he has limbs or has elbow room, but if he has mind free, and in what this consists.

Leibniz' own view is that the will can be 'inclined' but not 'necessitated'; that is to say, however much our reason and understanding may tell us to do something we are still free not to do it.

In the 18th century essentially the same view as Hobbes held was again affirmed by David Hume. But Hume goes further in showing how freedom, or 'liberty', and necessity can be reconciled. Hume's innovation is to argue that the 'necessary connection' which exists between causes and their effects is in fact no more than a uniform, constant conjunction between events:

> Our idea, therefore, of necessity and causation arises entirely from the uniformity observable in the operations of nature, where similar objects are constantly conjoined together, and the mind is determined by custom to infer the one from the appearance of the other. These two circumstances form the whole of that necessity which we ascribe to matter. Beyond the constant *conjunction* of similar objects and the consequent *inference* from one to the other, we have no notion of any necessity of connection.

Given this view of 'necessity' Hume sees no difficulty in reconciling it with 'liberty':

> But to proceed in this reconciling project with regard to the question of liberty and necessity – the most contentious question of metaphysics, the most contentious science – it will not require many words to prove that all mankind have ever agreed in the doctrine of liberty as well as in that of necessity, and that the whole dispute, in this respect also, has been hitherto merely verbal. For what is meant by liberty when applied to voluntary actions? We cannot surely mean that actions have so little connection with motives, inclinations, and circumstances that one does not follow with a certain degree of uniformity from the other, and that one affords no inference by which we can conclude the existence of the other. For these are plain and acknowledged matters of fact. By liberty, then, we can only mean *a power of acting or not acting according to the determinations of the will*; that is, if we choose to remain at rest, we may; if we choose to move, we also may. Now this hypothetical liberty is universally allowed to belong to everyone who is not a prisoner and in chains. Here then is no subject of dispute.

However, Hume's view of necessity and causation has been much disputed. Many philosophers think that the necessities in nature go beyond uniformity and constant conjunction. Consider, for instance, the law of gravity. On Hume's interpretation, this law states that as a matter of fact physical bodies just do attract each other depending on their mass and distance. But Hume's critics say that the law actually goes further: it says how things *must* happen, not just how they actually *do* happen. In particular, there's *nothing we can do* to change the law of gravity or make any exception to it; we are powerless. So if *our* existence is governed by scientific laws then we are powerless to change these laws too.

Immanuel Kant (also 18th century) rejected Hume's view of necessity and causation and his view that freedom could be reconciled with necessity. A crucial distinction in Kant's thought is the distinction between *autonomy* and *heteronomy.* To be free is to be autonomous; to be necessitated by external causes is to be heteronomous, therefore not free:

> As the will is a kind of causality of living beings in so far as they are rational, freedom would be that property of this causality by

which it can be effective independently of outside causes determining it, just as natural necessity is the property of the causality of all non-rational beings by which they are determined in their activity by the influence of outside causes.

The preceding definition of freedom is negative and therefore affords no insight into its essential nature. But a positive concept of freedom flows from it, which is so much the richer and more fruitful...Natural necessity is, as we have seen, a heteronomy of efficient causes, for every effect is possible only according to the law that something else determines the efficient cause to its causality. What else, then, can the freedom of the will be but autonomy, i.e. the property of the will to be a law to itself?

Thus, for Kant, there are two sorts of law. One sort of law governs the behaviour of non-rational beings (e.g. inanimate objects). This sort of law is 'empirical', that is, discoverable by observation. The other sort of law applies to rational beings, like ourselves, and is discoverable by reason. As rational beings, we decide *for ourselves* and therefore we cannot regard ourselves as heteronomous:

Reason must regard itself as the author of its principles, independently of outside influences; consequently, as practical reason or as the will of a rational being, it must regard itself as free. That is to say, the will of a rational being can be a will of its own only under the idea of freedom, and therefore in a practical point of view such a will must be ascribed to all rational beings.

In Kant's view the mistake made by Hume is to try to fit our freedom into the empirical world governed by scientific laws. But this is impossible. What we must recognize is that there are two standpoints from which to regard ourselves, (1) as belonging to the world of the senses, of 'appearance', governed by natural laws, and (2) as belonging to the 'intelligible' world, i.e. the world of understanding, governed by laws of reason. But what is the relation between these standpoints?

If the part of us that exists in the 'intelligible' world were separate from the part of us that exists in the world of 'sense', then we would have Descartes' dualism of a free self and a physical body. But what if the rational self is the *same* as the physical body, though viewed in a different way (as Spinoza thought)? The idea of a free self with a body governed by natural laws would then appear contradictory. As Kant says, 'it would be impossible to escape this contradiction if the subject, who seems to himself free, thought of himself in the same sense or in the same way when he calls himself free as when he assumes that in the same action he is subject to natural law'. How then can one avoid a contradiction without resorting to Cartesian dualism?

Kant's solution is to distinguish between ourselves as *appearances*, objects in the world of sense, and ourselves *as we are in ourselves:*

> Man, who in this way regards himself as intelligence, puts himself in a different order of things and relates himself to determining grounds of an altogether different kind when he thinks of himself as intelligence with a will and as thus endowed ·with causality, compared with that other order of things and that other set of determining grounds which become relevant when he perceives himself as a phenomenon in the world of sense (*as he really also is*) and submits his causality to external determination according to natural laws. Now he soon realizes that both can subsist together – indeed, that they must. For there is not the least contradiction between *a thing in appearance* (as belonging to the world of sense) being subject to certain laws of which it is independent *as a thing or a being in itself*. (My emphasis.)

This amounts to a sort of middle way between Descartes and Spinoza, but unfortunately it leaves obscure what the relationship is between ourselves as we are in ourselves and ourselves as we appear. In particular, Kant's account leaves us with the feeling that, unless we follow Descartes, we must conclude that in our case at least the appearances are *false* or else freedom can, after all, be reconciled with necessity.

The theme of freedom and necessity runs through the writings of 17th and 18th century philosophers, as we have seen. But different philosophers use the terms 'freedom' and 'necessity' in different ways. Some think of freedom as the freedom to do what one wants; others think of freedom as a special power of the will. Some think of necessity as natural necessity: what happens in accordance with scientific laws of nature is necessary. But Locke contrasts necessity with what is in one's power; thus a stone necessarily falls to the ground because it is not within its power to stop itself. And Hume thought that what we call the necessary connection of cause and effect is in fact only a uniform, constant conjunction.

Clearly, then, it is impossible to say whether freedom can be reconciled with necessity until we know what is meant by 'freedom', and what is meant by 'necessity'.

20th century philosophy

In this century the debate started in the 17th and 18th centuries has continued, and the influence of the older writers is often evident. There are Cartesians, Humeans, Kantians, and so on. Indeed, Plato, Aristotle and Aquinas are also influential (deservedly in my opinion).

Most of this book will be concerned with contemporary discussions of free will, so I shall not try to summarise these discussions here. One striking 20th century contribution to our topic does deserve special mention, however. That is Sartre's existentialism.

In his major existentialist work *Being and Nothingness (L'Etre et Le Néant)*, Sartre argues that we are 'condemned to be free', although in 'bad faith' (*mauvaise foi*) we try to deny our freedom and see ourselves as simply cogs in a machine, determined by outside forces. In fact, Sartre says, nothing determines anything we do unless we choose that it should.

Sartre perceptively notes that human beings tend to view motives as external forces prodding them into action. We disclaim responsibility for our motives and say we had 'no choice' but to do what we do. In Sartre's view this is just bad faith; that is, we're deceiving ourselves about our own nature. We pretend that the factors which affect our behaviour have a weight and importance independently of us; but actually they have no weight or importance apart from what we assign to them.

Sartre makes a fundamental distinction between two sorts of existing things, the 'for itself' (*pour soi*) and the 'in itself' (*en soi*). The *pour soi* exists 'for itself', that is to say, it is conscious of itself. The *en soi* lacks consciousness; it just exists. Sartre's notion of the *'pour soi'* recalls Descartes' Mind and Kant's autonomous Self.

Conscious beings like ourselves are necessarily free, in Sartre's view, because we can choose what and who to be. We are not constrained by what actually exists; we can think of what does not exist and turn it into reality, or think of what does exist and turn it into 'nothingness'. Sartre gives this example:

> A worker in 1830 is capable of revolting if his salary is lowered, for he easily conceives of a situation in which his wretched standard of living would be not as low as the one which is about to be imposed on him. But he does not represent his sufferings to himself as unbearable; he adapts himself to them not through resignation but because he lacks the education and reflection necessary for him to conceive of a social state in which these sufferings would not exist. Consequently *he* does not act...He suffers without considering his suffering and without conferring value upon it...Therefore this suffering cannot be in itself a motive for his acts. Quite the contrary, it is after he has formed the project of changing the situation that it will appear intolerable to him.

In order to change the situation the worker 'must posit an ideal state of affairs as a pure *present* nothingness', i.e. the state of affairs envisaged is not what presently exists, and he 'must posit the actual situation as nothingness in relation to this state of affairs', i.e. the present situation must *cease* to exist so that the future state of affairs may exist.

Existentialism is sometimes summed up in the epigram 'existence precedes essence', meaning that the fact that we exist precedes *what we are*, because we make of ourselves what we are, i.e. we become what we choose to be. The only thing we do not choose is our freedom; we are *necessarily* free. In *Existentialism and Humanism* Sartre provides this explanation:

> What is meant here by saying that existence precedes essence? It means that, first of all, man exists, turns up, appears on the scene, and, only afterwards, defines himself. If man, as the existentialist conceives him, is indefinable, it is because at first he is nothing. Only afterward will he be something, and he himself will have made what he will be. Thus, there is no human nature, since there is no God to conceive it. Not only

is man what he conceives himself to be, but he is also only what he wills himself to be after this thrust toward existence.

Man is nothing else but what he makes of himself. Such is the first principle of existentialism. It is also what is called subjectivity, the name we are labelled with when charges are brought against us. But what do we mean by this, if not that man has a greater dignity than a stone or table? For we mean that man first exists, that is, that man first of all is the being who hurls himself toward a future and who is conscious of imagining himself as being in the future. Man is at the start a plan which is aware of itself, rather than a patch of moss, a piece of garbage, or a cauliflower; nothing exists prior to this plan; there is nothing in heaven; man will be what he will have planned to be...Now, if existence really does precede essence, man is responsible for what he is. Thus, existentialism's first move is to make every man aware of what he is and to make the full responsibility of his existence rest on him.

The idea of self-creation is attractive. But there seems to be a problem: if our nature consists of nothing but the ability to choose, then how do we decide what is *best for us*? Do I not have to be a being of a certain sort for one thing to be better for me than another is? But if I *am* a being of a certain sort, then I do not, on Sartre's view, possess perfect freedom. If we do not possess perfect freedom, perhaps we are not as radically different from the rest of nature as Sartre suggests.

Sartre is right to think that human freedom and consciousness are intertwined. We do seem to have a perfect freedom of *imagination*, if not of will. At one point Sartre says: 'In a certain sense I choose being born.' We can imagine not being born; but we cannot will not to have been born. If we did not have the power to imagine what exists as non-existent and what is non-existent as existing, it does not seem possible that we could have free will.

notes

Socrates, 470-399 B.C. Greek philosopher and teacher of Plato. Sentenced to death in Athens for 'corrupting the youth', and died by drinking hemlock (see Plato's *Apology* and *Phaedo*). The quotation is from Plato's *Protagoras*, p. 358. Another of Plato's 'Socratic' dialogues which discusses whether 'virtue is knowledge' is the *Meno*.

Plato, 428-347 B.C. Greek philosopher. Many of his earlier works provide an interesting picture of Socrates; but his later works present his own philosophical views. The quotation is from the *Republic* (a long work portraying the ideal society), Bk 4, pp. 441-2.

Aristotle, 384-322 B.C. Greek philosopher. Wrote extensively in all the major areas of philosophy. The quotations are from his *Nicomachean Ethics*, Bk. 3, chs. 1 and 5.

Plotinus, 205-70 A.D. Studied in Alexandria and Rome. The quotation is from his *Enneads*, Bk. 3.

St. Augustine, 354-430 A.D. Christian philosopher. Author of *The City of God* and *On Free Will*. Augustine held that God's foreknowledge of our actions is compatible with free will (see ch. 5, Fourth Reason).

St. Thomas Aquinas, 1224-74. Italian philosopher and theologian. His major work is the *Summa Theologiae* (or *Summa Theologica*). Quotations are from Bk. 1, Ques. 83, Arts. 1 and 3.

René Descartes, 1596-1650. French philosopher, moved to Holland 1628. Considered to be one of the founders of modern philosophy. In his *Meditations* he sought to establish philosophy on absolutely certain principles. Descartes is probably best known for his saying, 'Cogito, ergo sum': 'I think, therefore I am.' The quotations are from his fourth *Meditation*.

Baruch Spinoza, 1632-77. Dutch philosopher. In his *Ethics* he sets out an entire system of philosophy *in more geometrico*, i.e. in the manner of Euclid's geometry: from various sets of definitions and axioms he deduces the propositions which constitute his philosophical system. Fortunately, the text is interspersed with notes and prefaces which are far easier to follow than his deductions. The quotations are from the Note to Proposition II, Part III, and from the Preface to Part V of the *Ethics*. Much of this work is concerned with the emotions. Part IV is entitled 'Of Human Bondage or the Strength of the Emotions', a title borrowed by Somerset Maugham for one of his novels.

Thomas Hobbes, 1588-1679, English philosopher. Held a materialistic view of human nature: only matter exists and the whole of human nature can be understood in mechanistic terms. Author of *Leviathan*, in which he constructs a political theory on the basis of his view of human nature. His debate with Bishop Bramhall, *The Questions concerning Liberty, Necessity, and Chance*, was published in 1656. It can be found in Volume V of Hobbes' collected works.

John Locke, 1632-1704. English philosopher. Author of *An Essay Concerning Human Understanding* (1690), in which he sets out a comprehensive theory that is the philosophical counterpart of the mechanical science which Boyle, Newton and others were creating in the 17th century. Locke is also noted for his contributions to political philosophy. Quotations are from Book II, ch. 21, secs. 9, 14, 27, of the *Essay.*

Gottfried Wilhelm Leibniz, 1646-1716. German philosopher and logician. His *New Essays on the Understanding* (1704) are a response to Locke's *Essay*. Quotations are from Book II, ch. 21, secs. 8, 21. Leibniz is probably best known for his saying that 'this is the best of all possible worlds'. Leibniz held the Principle of Sufficient Reason, according to which there must be a sufficient reason for everything which exists. Since there could be no reason for God, being all-knowing, all-powerful and perfectly good, to create a less than perfect world, this must be the best of all possible worlds. This is sometimes called the 'Panglossian' view after Dr. Pangloss in Voltaire's *Candide*, a satire on Leibniz' saying.

David Hume, 1711-76. Scottish philosopher. Author of the *Treatise on Human Nature* in three volumes, in which he presents a thoroughgoing empiricist philosophy. (For a brief description of empiricism see the glossary.) Hume is thought by many to be the greatest British philosopher; he is certainly one of the most influential. His later works, the *Enquiry Concerning Human Understanding* and the *Enquiry Concerning the Principles of Morals*, provide a further, more approachable, exposition of his views. The quotations are from 'Of Liberty and Necessity' Part I, in the *Enquiry Concerning Human Understanding.*

Immanuel Kant, 1724-1804. German philosopher. Kant's major, and difficult, works are the *Critique of Pure Reason* and the *Critique of Practical Reason*. But he also wrote some shorter and somewhat easier works, including the *Foundations of the Metaphysics of Morals*, which is not as forbidding as its title might suggest. In this work Kant argues that there is a 'categorical imperative' which is unconditionally binding on all rational creatures. This imperative is: 'Act only according to that maxim which you can at the same time will to be a universal law.' For instance, if you intend to act on the maxim, 'It's all right for me to lie', then you must will that as a universal law everyone should lie.   If you cannot rationally will this, then you should not lie. Quotations are from the third section of the *Foundations*.

Jean-Paul Sartre, 1905-80. French philosopher and novelist. Quotations are from his *Being and Nothingness* Pt. 4, ch. 1, secs. 1 and 2, and from his essay *Existentialism and Humanism*.

3: first reason for not believing in free will: all our choices and actions are causally determined

In this and the following two chapters we shall look at eighteen reasons for believing that we do not have free will. Historically the first of these reasons is the most important; and it will occupy us for two chapters. It presents a fundamental challenge to those who do believe in free will. In fact one's attitude to the whole free will question is likely to depend on whether one believes this challenge can be met and, if so, how. The First Reason (henceforth capitalised for convenience, as will be all the succeeding Reasons) is given two chapters because the discussion in the next chapter goes into the question in more detail and can be skipped on first reading by those who want a quick run-through of all the Reasons.

The First Reason says that (1) all our choices and actions are causally determined and (2) because of this fact we do not have free will. It thus contains two elements, which are distinct from each other. That is to say, it is quite possible to believe one and not the other. We cannot assume that if one is correct the other is also. And someone who accepts the First Reason must show that *both* elements are correct.

Holbach's statement of the first reason
The First Reason is accepted as a good reason for rejecting free will by B.F. Skinner (see chapter 1) and by Spinoza (see chapter 2), although both allow a sort of freedom: freedom from aversive stimuli (Skinner), freedom from the bondage of

emotion (Spinoza). The First Reason was also accepted by Baron d'Holbach (in the 18th century). He provides a forceful statement which is worth quoting at length. Holbach believes that 'man is a being purely physical':

> in whatever manner he is considered, he is connected to universal nature, and submitted to the necessary and immutable laws that she imposes on all the beings she contains, according to their particular essences or to the respective properties with which, without consulting them, she endows each particular species. Man's life is a line that nature commands him to describe upon the surface of the earth, without his ever being able to swerve from it, even for an instant. He is born without his own consent; his constitution in no way depends upon himself; his ideas come to him involuntarily; his habits are in the power of those who cause him to contract them; he is unceasingly modified by causes, whether visible or concealed, over which he has no control, which necessarily regulate his mode of existence, give the hue to his way of thinking, and determine his manner of acting.

Holbach thus wishes to argue that (a) human beings are wholly physical, (b) therefore they are wholly governed by physical laws, (c) therefore they are governed by causes over which 'they have no control'. Holbach sees the will as passive rather than active:

> This will is necessarily determined by the qualities, good or bad, agreeable or painful, of the object or motive which acts upon his senses, or of which the idea remains with him and is resuscitated by his memory. In consequence he acts necessarily, his action is the result of the impulse he receives either from the motive, from the object, or from the idea which has modified his brain, or disposed his will. When he does not act according to this impulse, it is because there comes some new cause, some new motive, some new idea, which modifies his brain in a different manner, gives him a new impulse, determines his will in another way, by which the action of the former impulse is suspended.

It is no argument against this to say that sometimes we act against our inclinations:

> Man, it is said, frequently acts against his inclination, from which it is falsely concluded he is a free agent; but when he

appears to act contrary to his inclination, he is always determined to it by some motive sufficiently efficacious to vanquish
this inclination. A sick man, with a view to his cure, arrives at
conquering his repugnance to the most disgusting remedies.
The fear of pain, or the dread of death, then become necessary
motives; consequently this sick man cannot be said to act freely.

Holbach totally rejects Hume's attempt to reconcile freedom
and necessity:

The partisans of the system of free agency appear always to
have confused constraint and necessity. Man believes he acts
as a free agent every time he sees nothing which places
obstacles to his actions. He does not see that the motive which
causes him to will is always necessary and independent of
himself. A prisoner loaded with chains is compelled to remain
in prison; but he is not a free agent in the desire to emancipate
himself.

Just as external obstacles prevent us from acting otherwise than
we do, so internal factors prevent us from choosing otherwise
than we do.

Like Spinoza, Holbach thinks that the belief that our choices
and actions are not governed by universal laws is the result of
ignorance. Holbach concedes that the causes of our actions
are not simple and obvious; but it does not follow that they do
not exist:

It is the great complication of motion in man, the vanity of his
action, the multiplicity of causes which move him, whether
simultaneously or in continual succession, that persuade him
he is a free agent. If all his motions were simple, if the causes
that move him did not get mixed up together, if they were
distinct, if his mechanism were less complicated, he would
perceive that all his actions are necessary because he would be
able to recur instantly to the cause which made him act.

This, however, perhaps invites the reply that complicated
mechanisms like us *can* have free will, though no doubt simple
mechanisms cannot.

To summarize: Holbach provides the following reasons in
favour of believing that (1) all our choices and actions are
causally determined:
(a) we are purely physical; therefore

(b) we are governed by physical necessity in accordance with universal physical laws (whether we know it or not).

And he provides the following reasons in favour of believing that (2) because of this fact we do not have free will:

(a) the causes of our choices and actions are outside our control;

(b) we do not have the power to act against our motives (one motive can only be overcome by another motive, and the second is as much outside our control as the first);

(c) it is not sufficient for free will that we are free from external obstacles (we must have power over our motives as well as over external obstacles).

These are Holbach's reason's for not believing in free will. Are they good reasons? Let us look more closely at the statements we have numbered (1) and (2).

(1) all our choices and actions are causally determined

Statement (1) is an application of the thesis of *determinism* to human choices and actions. We have been talking rather vaguely about causes and scientific laws. We must now be more specific.

Determinism is sometimes summed up in two sentences: 'Every event has a cause' and 'Same cause, same effect.'

First, *nothing is uncaused*. We may not know the cause but there always is one.

Second, the cause must be a *sufficient* cause: whenever the cause is present the effect follows. An event cannot be the sufficient cause of an effect it sometimes fails to produce.

To give an example: striking a match might cause a flame on one occasion but not on another. So striking the match is not by itself a sufficient cause; it must also be the case that the match is dry, that oxygen is present, etc. Given all these conditions we then have a sufficient cause, such that if the cause is present then the effect occurs.

When the cause is a sufficient cause, the statement 'If the cause is present, the effect occurs' is universally true. It thus constitutes a *law of nature*. For instance, the statement 'If metal is heated, it expands' relates a cause and an effect. If the cause is a sufficient cause of the effect, then universally, in all cases, the cause will be followed by the effect: if the metal actually is heated, it will expand; and if metal which is not actually heated were to be heated, it would expand. If all this holds, then the statement 'If metal is heated, it expands' expresses a law of nature.

It is the universality of laws of nature which constitutes natural necessity. Events necessarily occur in conformity with the laws of nature because there are no exceptions to those laws. Things must happen as the law says they do (or else it is not a true law of nature). Thus, when an effect is causally determined in accordance with a law of nature, it is *causally necessitated.*

A law of nature is thus quite different from a generalization which merely happens to be true. It is not a law of nature that men should go out to work and women should stay at home, though in a given society it might be true that no women went out to work and no men stayed at home. The generalization 'Men go out to work and women stay at home' would be true in that society; but it would not be a law of nature since it is not true in other societies.

We have seen that if determinism is true there must be laws of nature. Physics is the science which more than any other attempts to formulate laws of nature, e.g. the law of gravity. In other sciences laws are not so easy to come by. In psychology, for instance, it is hard to state any hard and fast laws which are informative. I might say 'If someone wants something more than she wants anything else, then she acts so as to get that thing'. But this is obviously not a *law*. Too many things can interfere and prevent her from acting so as to get that thing: she may not be able to do what is required (she may want a computer more than anything else but not have the money to buy one), she may not have the opportunity to do it (she is living at the North Pole), she may change her mind ('who needs a computer?'), she may be physically prevented (run over on the way to buy it), etc. Obviously it is very hard to frame a law which will rule out all the interfering factors; but it is only when they are ruled out that we can formulate a deterministic law.

By the principle of 'Same cause, same effect' we must exclude all the factors which prevent the same cause from being followed by the same effect.

In psychology we find researchers looking for statistical correlations rather than laws. That is to say, they look for cases where there is a high probability or likelihood of one thing following another. Underlying such correlations they expect to find cause and effect relationships, even though they cannot actually formulate a deterministic law. The same thing happens, of course, in other sciences. For instance, smoking cigarettes is not a sufficient cause of getting lung cancer since not every case of smoking leads to lung cancer. But there is a higher probability of a smoker getting lung cancer than of a non-smoker getting it; so researchers infer that there is a causal relation between smoking and lung cancer.

Does the difficulty, or even the impossibility, of discovering psychological laws show that human psychology is not deterministic? Not necessarily. The fact is that physics has advantages which other sciences do not; so we should expect physics rather than the other sciences to come up with laws of nature, even if all the sciences are deterministic. First, the factors which can interfere to prevent a physical cause producing a certain effect are already provided for in physical laws without having to be listed individually. To give a simple example: a certain force may cause a certain object to move a certain distance, but not if another force is acting on that object from the opposite direction. The same physical law which explains why the effect occurs in the first case *also* explains why it does not occur in the second.

Physics is the *basic* science. Human beings have a psychology, but we are also physical beings. A whole host of physical factors can interfere with our psychological lives, from brain damage to hurricanes. It is thus impossible to give a complete account of our psychology which does not also bring in physics. But a complete account of our physical nature does not need to bring in any other science. Physics thus has an advantage over other sciences: they need it, but it doesn't need them.

So the non-existence of psychological laws does not prove that psychology is not deterministic. But do we have any proof that it *is* deterministic? Perhaps there are no deterministic relationships underlying the statistical correlations which psychologists study? In that case something like Leibniz' position would be vindicated: we are 'inclined' but not 'necessitated'.

Descartes clearly thought that our Minds are not governed by deterministic relationships. Holbach, of course, thinks that Cartesian dualism is a mistake: Mind is not separate from Body; 'man is a being purely physical' and thus wholly governed by physical, deterministic laws. However, we cannot take it for granted that mental processes are *not* deterministic or that physical processes *are* deterministic.

According to Heisenberg's Principle of Indeterminacy, at the level of the elementary particles which constitute matter physics is not deterministic. Einstein objected to this idea on the ground that 'God does not play dice'. But perhaps God does, at least when it doesn't matter. Indeterminism in quantum physics (the science of elementary particles) would be insignificant if indeterminism at the subatomic level co-exists with determinism at the level of 'macroscopic' (observable) objects.

But there may conceivably also be indeterminism at the 'macro' level. Such indeterminism would not prove that we do have free will. If the indeterminism were totally freakish and random, quite independent of our reason and will, it would count against free will, not in its favour. But if there were an indeterminism in our choices and actions, that would be enough to undermine Holbach's argument for the First Reason. Is there?

Holbach sees human action in billiard ball terms. A motive or impulse comes along and impels the agent in one direction, unless another motive comes along and impels him in another. But we must bear in mind Sartre's caution against supposing that a motive has a force or weight independently of that which the agent assigns to it. Holbach emphasizes that human beings necessarily pursue certain goals. In order to understand that human actions are necessitated, 'It suffices to know that, by his essence, man tends to conserve himself, and to render his existence happy'. However, it is fallacious to infer the necessitation of human actions from the necessity of human goals, as Aquinas makes clear. Aquinas argued (a) that 'the will of necessity cleaves to its final fulfilment, happiness', but also (b) that 'the will does not by necessity will whatever it wills':

> The will can tend towards nothing that is not conceived to be good. But because there are many kinds of good thing it is not by any necessity determined to any particular one.

Thus, more than the necessity of our ultimate goals is required in order to prove the necessity of our actions.

However, even if Holbach has not succeeded in proving that human psychology is deterministic, his conclusion is nevertheless plausible. For example, if two people are exposed to the same temptation and if each is similarly attracted to it, but one succumbs and the other does not, we generally assume that there was some factor present in the one case and not in the other which explains the difference in outcome. Unfortunately, the fact that we assume determinism (supposing we do) in no way shows that determinism is correct.

Determinism is a methodological assumption, the value of which lies in the discoveries we have made about the world around us. It cannot be conclusively verified or falsified. However many causes we turn up, that does not absolutely prove that *everything* has a cause. And however much we fail to discover something's cause, that does not absolutely prove that it has *no* cause. But our acceptance of determinism is by no means unjustified.

Some philosophers have held that it is a necessary truth, knowable through the use of our reason, independently of any empirical observation, that every event has a sufficient cause. But the fact is that, however hard it may be for us to conceive of something happening without there being a sufficient cause for its happening, it is nevertheless quite *possible*.

Determinism is not a truth discernible by the use of reason alone. It is an assumption about the world which, generally speaking, does appear to be a fact. However, if we find that there are good reasons for believing our choices and actions to be exempt from determinism, then we shall have to revise our assumption. And we must not forget that Descartes and Kant reject the idea that determinism applies to our choices and actions.

(2) because of this fact, we do not have free will

We must now inquire whether statement (2) is correct: does the truth of determinism applied to our choices and actions imply that we have no free will?

Holbach thinks it does because he believes that if determinism is correct, then our actions are caused by our wills and our wills are caused by our motives and our motives are caused by external factors over which we have no control and/or by our internal organization over which, again, we have no control. If determinism is true, there is a *chain* of causes and effects extending back in time from our actions into the indefinite past. It is obvious that we have no control over the past; we cannot change that. Since we have no control over the past causes of our actions, it follows, according to Holbach, that we have no free will.

This argument is certainly appealing. We know that we are products ultimately of a past in which we did not exist and that we did not create ourselves. If determinism applies to *every* facet of ourselves, how is anything *our* doing, rather than simply the product of past causes?

Holbach is surely right when he says that we do not have free will in respect to those things over which we do not have control. For instance, I certainly do not have free will as regards past events; I cannot choose my parents, for example. Again, I certainly do not have free will as regards laws of nature; I cannot choose to violate the law of gravity, for example. I cannot work miracles, in the strict sense according to which a 'miracle' is an exception to the laws of nature and thus requires 'supernatural' powers. So I do not have the powers that God has. God is not limited by laws of nature at all. His omnipotence extends to changing the laws of nature if he wants to.

When Descartes says that in the freedom of his will he re-sembles God, he means, not that he Descartes can change the laws of nature, but that his will is not determined in conformity with laws of nature, just as God's is not. Now, if our wills are in fact determined, then it is clear that we lack a freedom which God has, namely the freedom of a will which is not determined in accordance with laws of nature. If the only freedom which people think worthwhile is freedom from being determined in accordance with laws of nature, then, if our wills are determined, we obviously lack that freedom.

But is that the only freedom which is worthwhile? Surely not – unless being determined in accordance with the laws of nature means that we do not have free will at all.

Holbach is right to say that we do not have free will in regard to those things which are outside our control; so he must also be right to say that, if we do not have control over our motives and if our wills are necessarily determined by our motives, we do not have free will at all. But why does he say that we do not have control over our motives?

If his reasoning is that our motives are the effects of causes over which we have no control and hence it follows that we have no control over our motives, then his reasoning is faulty. For he would be depending on the principle, 'What is caused by factors outside our control is itself outside our control'. And this is false as a general principle: an event outside our control brings about an effect which is also outside our control, only if we have no control over whether it brings about that effect.

The best way of showing that a principle is not generally valid is to find a counter-example. Here is one: suppose I am forcibly dragged onto an aeroplane, the plane takes off, a parachute is strapped onto me, and then one mile high I am pushed out of the plane. This whole sequence is out of my control. Furthermore, pushing me out of the plane will, if I do not open the parachute, cause my death or at least serious injury. Suppose further that, perversely, I do not open my parachute. Then pushing me out of the plane causes my death or serious injury. But this result was *not* outside my control. If I had opened the parachute, which was fully operational and under my control, I would not have been killed or seriously injured. Thus it is not true that what is caused by factors outside our control must itself be outside our control.

Of course if I had not had the parachute on when I was pushed out of the plane, it *would* have been out of my control whether I was killed or seriously injured. In that situation there would have been nothing that I could have done to prevent this result. But this confirms, rather than refutes, the conclusion that in the first sort of case we do have control over whether an event outside our control leads to a certain result.

The difference between the first case and the second is that in the first the causal factors outside my control do *not* causally necessitate the effect, whereas in the second they do. In the first case it is the causal factors outside my control *plus* my refraining from doing anything which together necessitate the effect. But since I can prevent what would otherwise happen from happening, the effect is not outside my control. In the second case, the causal factors outside my control do causally necessitate the effect, and so the effect is outside my control.

When we say that something is 'out of our control', we mean that whatever we may try to do, we cannot change the outcome or affect what happens. If I jump out of a high window without a parachute or rope or other support, it is out of my control whether I fall downwards; whatever I may try to do, I shall still fall downwards. Now, if this is what is meant by 'out of our control', then our motives are not out of our control. We believe that if we try hard we can overcome our motives, sometimes at least. Perhaps *some* motives, e.g. the motive of self-preservation in the face of life-threatening disaster, are literally irresistible. But this does not mean that all motives are.

Let us consider what Holbach has to say about this (I have recast it into dialogue form for clarity):

"Is a human being the master of desiring or not desiring an object which appears desirable to him?"

"No; but he is the master of resisting his desire, if he reflects on the consequences."

"But is he capable of reflecting on these consequences, when his soul is hurried along by a lively passion, which entirely depends on his nature and on external causes? Is it in his power to add to these consequences all the weight necessary to counterbalance his desire?"

"He ought to have learned to resist his passions, to have acquired a habit of curbing his desires."

"I agree; but is his nature capable of such modification? Does his fiery and impetuous nature allow him to apply true knowledge at the moment it is needed? And even if his temperament

> makes that possible, have his education and upbringing
> equipped him to acquire this habit of repressing his desires?"

Holbach here describes someone who *cannot*, for one reason
or another, resist a desire. But the fact that some cannot does
not show that no one can resist a desire or motive. Holbach
has not shown that everyone is incapable of reflecting on the
consequences, that everyone has a headstrong temperament
(he explicitly concedes this), or that everyone has had a terrible
education or upbringing. All he is entitled to conclude is that
someone who cannot resist a desire has been caused not to
resist it. But what he needs, to prove his point, is that everyone
who has been caused not to resist a desire is incapable of
resisting it. But the second statement does not follow from the
first, at least not without some further argument.

Now, the optimistic view which Holbach is attacking may
be a mistake. But statement (2) is not obviously true.
Holbach's argument needs further support. And indeed many
arguments have been proposed to show that statement (2) is
true.

It has seemed to many that if determinism is true then we
cannot choose to do anything other than what we do choose to
do. Again, it has seemed that if determinism is true, then we
never really originate anything, because we are only products
of our pasts. But free will means that we *can* choose to do
what we do not in fact choose to do and that we *are* originators
of our actions. So, if determinism applies to our choices and
actions, then we do not have free will.

But many others are not convinced. They think that we have
free will even if determinism is true.

In the next chapter we shall look more closely at these
arguments. But this chapter can be omitted if you have had
enough of the First Reason for the time being.

notes

B. F. Skinner. See chs. 1 and 5 (Eighth Reason).

Holbach, Paul Henri Dietrich, Baron d', 1723-89. French philosopher and contributor to Diderot's *Encyclopaedia*. Exponent of atheism and materialism. His best known work is *The System of Nature* (1770). The quotations are from a translation of ch. 11: 'Of the System of Man's Free Agency'.

Descartes, Hume, Kant, Leibniz, Spinoza. See ch. 2.

Determinism and Heisenberg's Principle. See S. Hook, ed., *Determinism and Freedom*, Pts. I and II, for further discussion.

Mind/Body Problem. See Geoffrey Brown's book in this series, *Minds, Brains and Machines*.

Sartre. See chs. 1 and 2.

Aquinas. See ch. 2. The quotations are from the *Summa Theologiae*, I, 82, arts. 1 and 2.

4: first reason for not believing in free will: further discussion

This chapter is a systematic and detailed discussion of issues raised by the First Reason. It is the most difficult chapter in the book, and may be omitted. However, I would be untrue to the history of our subject if I left out this material.

As well as airing some well-worn arguments about free will and determinism, I have made use of some terminology and technical apparatus which philosophers often use in presenting and examining arguments. These can seem tedious and tiresome to the newcomer (and, indeed, to veterans, though for different reasons). Their advantage is that they show precisely how a theorist is trying to establish a particular conclusion; and this can help the critic to see the various different questions which may be raised about the theorist's reasonings.

the first reason restated, and the three views about it
In the last chapter we stated the First Reason in this way: all our choices and actions are causally determined; because of this fact we do not have free will. This can be rephrased, a little more formally, as Argument A:

A (1) All our choices and actions are causally necessitated in accordance with deterministic laws.
  (2) If all our choices and actions are causally necessitated in accordance with deterministic laws, then we do not have free will.
Therefore,
  (3) We do not have free will.

This is what is known as a *valid deductive argument*. That is to say, it is an argument whose conclusion (3) follows logically from the premises (1 and 2). What this means is that it is impossible for the premises to be true but the conclusion not true; so that to accept the premises as true but reject the conclusion would be self-contradictory. Now, a valid argument does not by itself prove that the conclusion is true. In order for an argument to prove that the conclusion is true, not only must the argument be valid, the premises must be true. A valid deductive argument with true premises is called a *sound* deductive argument.

We already noted, in chapter 3, that there are *two* elements in the First Reason. Our argument A shows this clearly by having two premises (1 and 2), both of which must be true in order to prove the conclusion true.

Since Argument A is valid, someone who accepts the premises must accept the conclusion. Conversely, someone who rejects the conclusion must reject one or both of the premises. Historically, three positions have been held concerning Argument A. First, there are those who accept both premises and therefore also the conclusion. They are called *Hard Determinists*. Second, there are those who accept premise (1) but reject the conclusion (3). They therefore reject premise (2). They are called *Soft Determinists*. Like the Hard Determinists they accept determinism, but take a 'softer' line, thinking that determinism can be reconciled with free will. Third, there are those who reject the conclusion (3) but accept premise (2). Consequently, they reject premise (1). Unlike both Hard and Soft Determinists, they do not believe that our choices and actions are necessitated in accordance with deterministic laws. They are called *Libertarians*.

You will notice that between any two of these views there is one point of agreement and two points of disagreement:

Hard Determinism agrees with Soft Determinism about (1), disagrees about (2) and (3).

Hard Determinism agrees with Libertarianism about (2), disagrees about (1) and (3).

Soft Determinism agrees with Libertarianism about (3), disagrees about (1) and (2).

Thus the Soft Determinists and the Libertarians, both of whom reject the First Reason, do so for directly opposed reasons.

In order to decide which of these views is correct, we must examine Argument *A*. In particular we must consider whether its premises are true.

determinism (premise 1 of argument A)

In chapter 3 we discussed whether determinism is true. So far as I can see there is no way for a philosopher to prove that premise (1) is true. The only evidence for the truth of determinism is *empirical,* that is, based on observation and experiment. It would be possible for a philosopher to prove that premise (1) is false if he could prove that premise (2) is true and that the conclusion (3) is false. But that does not mean that it could ever be possible for a philosopher to prove that premise (1) is true. Thus I shall here look only at arguments to prove that premise (1) is false.

Libertarians reject premise (1) because they reject the conclusion of Argument *A* but accept that premise (2) is true. Some also reject premise (1) for religious reasons. They argue as follows.

(a) God punishes us for intentionally doing evil.

(b) It would be unfair of God to punish us for intentionally doing evil, if all our choices and actions are causally necessitated in accordance with deterministic laws.

(c) God does nothing unfair.

Therefore,

(d) It is not the case that all our choices and actions are causally necessitated in accordance with deterministic laws (i.e. premise 1 of Argument *A* is false).

However, this argument does not seem to add anything to their other argument since surely the only reason why premise (b) is true is that God would then be punishing us when we were not acting out of free will.

We are left, then, with the Libertarians' first argument which may be formulated thus:

(e) If all our choices and actions are necessitated in accordance with deterministic laws, then we do not have free will (= premise (2) of Argument *A*).

(f) We do have free will (i.e. conclusion of Argument *A* is false).

Therefore,

(g) It is not the case that all our choices and actions are causally necessitated in accordance with deterministic laws (i.e. premise (1) of Argument *A* is false).

This argument is valid, but, again, it only proves the conclusion if the premises are true. We'll look at premise (e) (= premise (2) of Argument *A*) in a minute. Libertarians must also show that we do have free will. They commonly try to do this by appealing to our consciousness of making a choice. They claim that we are conscious in making a choice that it is *our* choice and that we can definitely choose either to do or not to do whatever action we are deciding about (see the First Reason in favour of free will). They also claim that we have free will because we are morally responsible (see chapter 7).

There is a further challenge which Libertarians must face. They must explain how our choices and actions are truly *ours* if they are not causally determined. It might seem (and indeed has seemed to some critics) that if our choices and actions are not causally determined, then they just 'pop up' in a totally random, arbitrary and unpredictable way. But if choices just happen in this undetermined ('indeterministic') way, then what makes them *our* choices? What makes them the expression of *our* free will?

Libertarians reply that they are not defending indeterminism but *self*-determinism: the view that one's choices are determined by one's *self*. As Thomas Reid wrote (in the 18th century):

> a free action is an effect produced by a being who had power and will to produce it; therefore it is not an effect without a cause.

But what is this 'self' which is somehow exempt from deterministic processes? It sounds like Descartes' non-physical mind. Must we then support Cartesian dualism in order to be Libertarians?

It does seem difficult, perhaps impossible, to reconcile Libertarianism with the view that human beings are wholly physical in their constitution. According to Libertarianism, physical indeterminism without self-determinism is as incompatible with free will as is physical determinism. But unless the self is non-physical, the only difference between what self-determinism gives us and what a deterministic account can give us is physical indeterminism. So, unless the self is not physical, it would seem that self-determinism, like mere physical indeterminism, is not enough to give us any free will beyond what a deterministic account can give us. At all events, the Hard Determinist will obviously be unconvinced by the Libertarian's argument since the Hard Determinist rejects free will (premise f). In the Hard Determinist's view, Libertarianism is a fantasy, the fantasy of escaping determinism by supposing that human beings are somehow superior to everything else in the world and that we stand outside nature: we dictate to it but it does not dictate to us.

incompatibilism (premise (2) of argument A)

Those who say that premise (2) is true are called *Incompatibilists*, because they say that determinism is incompatible with free will, i.e. that determinism excludes free will and vice versa. Those who deny premise (2) are called *Compatibilists,* because they say that determinism is compatible with free will, i.e. both can co-exist together.

Hard Determinists and Libertarians are all Incompatibilists. Soft Determinists are Compatibilists. But a Compatibilist need not be a Soft Determinist: she might think that *both* premises (1 and 2) are false, or perhaps she just can't decide whether premise (1) is true, whereas a Soft Determinist accepts premise (1) as true. So Compatibilism is a very restricted thesis, it *only* concerns premise (2); it is not even really a positive thesis about whether we do have free will at all (though as a matter of fact all the Compatibilists I know of do think we have free will). Incompatibilists generally have strong positive views; they either deny free will (if they are Hard Determinists) or deny determinism (if they are Libertarians). But it is (just) possible to imagine an Incompatibilist who can't make up his mind: he knows he must reject either determinism or free will but he can't decide which.

In order to decide between Compatibilism and Incompatibilism we must see what reasons there are for rejecting or accepting premise (2). It is not self-evident, as we said in chapter 3, that if our choices and actions are causally necessitated in accordance with deterministic laws, then we do not have free will. But philosophers have thought that premise (2) can be shown to be true by further arguments whose premises we must accept.

These arguments generally have the following form: they state that if we have free will then such-and-such is the case, but if our actions are causally necessitated then such-and-such is *not* the case, from which we can infer that if our actions are causally necessitated then we do not have free will. Schematically:

If free will, then X is the case.

If determinism, then X is not the case.

Therefore, if determinism, then no free will.

So long as 'X' means the same thing in both premises this is a valid argument form: the conclusion follows logically from the premises.

can we act otherwise? (first argument for premise (2) of argument A)

Historically, the most important argument in favour of premise (2) is that if we have free will then we can act differently from the way we do act, but if determinism applies to our choices and actions then we can never do anything different from what we do do. More formally:

B (4) If we have free will, then we can act otherwise than we do act.

(5) If all our choices and actions are causally necessitated in accordance with deterministic laws, then it is not the case that we can act otherwise than we do act.

Therefore,

(2) If all our choices and actions are causally necessitated in accordance with deterministic laws, then we do not have free will.

Statement (2), which was a premise in Argument *A*, is the conclusion of Argument *B*.

The Compatibilist rejects the conclusion of Argument *B*; hence she must show that at least one of the premises is false or the argument is not in fact valid, despite appearances.

The only way in which Argument *B* could fail to be valid is if the phrase 'we cannot act otherwise than we do' has a different meaning in premise (4) from its meaning in premise (5). If this phrase is being used with different meanings in the two premises, this is called a fallacy of equivocation (or fallacy of ambiguity). A simple example of fallacy of equivocation is:

All rivers have banks.

Banks are places where people keep money.

Therefore, all rivers have places where people keep money. Obviously 'bank' means 'river bank' in the first premise and 'money bank' in the second. So the argument is not valid. Alternatively, if 'bank' means 'money bank' in both premises, then the first premise is obviously false.

What the Compatibilist wants to say is that if (4) and (5) are understood in such a way that they are both true, then the argument is invalid because of a fallacy of equivocation. Alternatively, if the fallacy of equivocation is eliminated (by ensuring that 'we can act otherwise than we do' has the same meaning in both premises), then at least one of the premises will be false. Either way the argument fails to prove the conclusion.

One standard way in which Compatibilists argue is to say that in premise (4) the phrase 'we can act otherwise than we do' means 'if we want (or choose) to act otherwise, then we will'. Now, if this is what 'we can act otherwise' means, then premise (5) is false, because it is quite compatible with determinism to say that if we have a different desire or make a different choice, then we will act differently from the way we actually do. To make (5) true we would have to give a different meaning to 'we can act otherwise'. According to the Compatibilist, there is no way of giving the same meaning to 'we can act otherwise' in both premises and producing a *sound* argument (one which is both valid and has true premises).

This Compatibilist argument has convinced some philosophers, for example Hume (see chapter 2), but it is open to objection.

The Incompatibilist can argue that there is not in fact a fallacy of equivocation at all. The phrase 'we can act otherwise than we do' means that it is in our power to act otherwise than we do. Now, if our choices and actions are causally necessitated, then it is not in our power to act otherwise, because it is impossible to avoid doing what is necessary.

The Incompatibilist offers this diagnosis of the Compatibilist's mistake: the Compatibilist sees that free will implies being able to act differently, but she interprets 'being able to act differently' in a very *narrow* way, a way which makes being able to act differently compatible with determinism, but which is only *part* of the story. The Compatibilist has selected only what fits in with her view and left out everything else (compare Bramhall on Hobbes, chapter 2).

The Compatibilist says that our having free will implies that we can act otherwise in the sense that if we want or choose to act differently, then, other things being equal, we will. But, the Incompatibilist argues, there is much more to being able to act differently than this. In the first place, it might not be possible for us to *want* or *choose* to act differently (compare Holbach, chapter 3). But, if so, then we would be unable to act differently. In the second place, acting differently might be impossible for us because it might involve violating a law of nature or changing the past, neither of which we can do. In this case, again, we would be unable to act otherwise.

Thus, according to the Incompatibilist, *three* conditions must be fulfilled for us to be able to act otherwise; and having free will implies being able to act otherwise in a sense which requires that all three of these conditions are fulfilled:

We are able to act otherwise if and only if

(i) we would act otherwise, other things being equal, if we wanted to; and

(ii) we are able to want to (or to choose to) act otherwise; and

(iii) acting otherwise would not involve doing something impossible like violating a law of nature or changing the past.

Once we give this fuller account of what 'we can act otherwise' means, the Incompatibilist view seems much more plausible.

How will the Compatibilist respond to this? She should, I think, concede that (ii), as well as (i), is required for free will. On this issue we should side with Descartes and Leibniz against Hobbes and Locke (see chapter 2). For if a person is unable to choose or want to act otherwise than he does (as is popularly supposed to be the case with, for example, drug addicts and those who have been hypnotised or brainwashed), then he certainly has no free will. But it is open to the Compatibilist to say that being able to want or choose otherwise means that if the person found the alternative course of action more attractive, he would want or choose that alternative. So long as it is true that the person would not in fact act, want, or choose differently unless some condition were fulfilled which is not in fact fulfilled, then there is no incompatibility with determinism. For instance, if being able to choose otherwise means that I would actually choose otherwise only if I had some different belief(s) instead of the one(s) I do have, then this is quite compatible with determinism, since determinism says that a certain choice is causally necessitated given the beliefs I have, *not* given different beliefs.

Consider a mundane example: I am driving my car along at 30 m.p.h. and I say to you 'This car can do 80 m.p.h.' You might retort 'No, it can't. According to the deterministic laws which govern this car's behaviour, with the conditions as they are, with the accelerator depressed just so far, in the gear that the car is in, etc., etc., it is causally necessary that it go at 30 m.p.h.; therefore, it *cannot* go at 80 m.p.h.' I may justifiably reply 'When I say it can go at 80 m.p.h., I do not mean that with all the conditions you have mentioned exactly as they are, it will sometimes do 80; that would offend against the principle of "Same cause, same effect". What I mean is that if the car is in top gear and the accelerator is depressed further than it is now and if the car is not going up a steep hill, etc., etc., it will go at 80 m.p.h.' Here we see clearly that for this car to go at 80 m.p.h. it is necessary that some condition be fulfilled which is not in fact fulfilled; and that is why it is quite compatible with determinism to say that this car, which is in fact going at 30 m.p.h., *can* go at 80.

What we have been saying not only indicates a way in which the Compatibilist can accept condition (ii), it also suggests that she can accept condition (iii). For if wanting, choosing, or acting otherwise requires that some condition, which is not in fact fulfilled, be fulfilled, then wanting, choosing, or acting otherwise would not in fact involve violating a law of nature or changing the past: if the agent were to make a different choice or perform a different action (different from his actual choice or action), that would imply a difference in the antecedent conditions. Just as the car in fact goes 80 only when some factor in the existing situation is changed (e.g. the accelerator is depressed further), so we agents would choose or act differently only if we knew something we don't actually know or if some other psychological or physical factor is different.

Now, the Incompatibilist will not accept this view of the situation. He will insist that, if actually making a different choice implies *a difference in the antecedent conditions*, then a person *cannot* choose differently *in the conditions as they are*. However, this argument is dismissed as fallacious by the Compatibilist. One might as well, she says, argue that a car *cannot* go faster than it *is* going *in the conditions as they are* because actually going faster implies some difference *from the conditions as they are*. To say that a car can go faster in the conditions as they are is to say that the existing conditions do not make it impossible to drive the car faster, as it would be if for instance the car were going at its maximum speed. Similarly, a person can choose to act differently if existing conditions do not make it impossible to choose differently, as it would be if for instance he were in a coma.

The Incompatibilist may reply that if determinism is true then existing conditions *always* make it impossible for a person to choose differently. But the Compatibilist rejects this thesis unless it just means that if determinism is true, then existing conditions plus the laws of nature lead to just one outcome (by the 'Same cause, same effect' principle); this is the only sense in which, according to the Compatibilist, premise (5) is true. Premise (5), understood in this way, does not make a different outcome *impossible*; it just implies that producing a different outcome involves altering existing conditions.

The Incompatibilist is unconvinced. He points out that, according to determinism, existing conditions are a product of past conditions, and past conditions together with the laws of nature imply that an agent will act in a certain way (do *X*, say). This means that if the agent *can* act otherwise than he does (i.e. not do *X*), then he must either be *able* to change the past conditions or violate the laws of nature. Since he *cannot* do either of these things, he *cannot* act otherwise. (You may by now be getting the impression that the argument is going round and round in the same tracks.)

How does the Compatibilist respond to this argument? She rejects the sentence in the last paragraph which begins 'This means'. It doesn't. The Incompatibilist is making a false supposition. He is supposing that if an agent can refrain from doing *X* and if refraining from doing *X* in the particular circumstances implies that either the past or the laws of nature are different from what they actually are, then that agent *can* either change the past or violate the laws of nature. But this supposition, though tempting, is mistaken.

If it were valid, one could equally argue that a human agent can deceive God. Suppose I will leave town tomorrow. Then God, being omniscient, knows that I will leave town tomorrow. Now, if I have free will, then I can refrain from leaving town tomorrow. But in that case I can deceive God. For if I can refrain from leaving town tomorrow, and if refraining from leaving town tomorrow in the particular circumstances implies that God is mistaken, then I can bring it about that God is mistaken. However I cannot (since God is omniscient). Hence the principle 'If an agent can do X, and if doing X in the particular circumstances implies doing Y, then that agent can do Y' is just not a valid principle. Even if acting differently from the way I actually act would in the particular circumstances imply that I am changing the past or violating the laws of nature, the fact that I cannot do either of these things does not imply that I cannot act differently.

summary of the discussion of argument B

The disagreement over whether or not Argument B is a good argument comes down to a disagreement over what it means to say that someone 'could have chosen, or acted, otherwise'. The Incompatibilist holds that no one could choose or act otherwise if determinism is true. The Compatibilist disagrees. She holds that for someone to be able to choose or act differently from the way he does, all that is necessary is that (1) the person is capable in general of making choices and acting in accordance with them, and (2) nothing is preventing the person from choosing or acting differently on the particular occasion in question; the existence of an unchangeable past and of deterministic laws does not prevent someone from choosing or acting differently.

The nub of the Incompatibilist case is that 'I could have chosen otherwise' means 'Given the circumstances as they were (without addition or subtraction) and given all the laws of nature as they are, my making a different choice was not causally excluded.' The Compatibilist agrees that, *if* this is what 'I could have chosen otherwise' means, then we cannot choose otherwise than we do, if determinism is true. But she insists that this is not the meaning of 'I could have chosen otherwise' which is relevant for free will.

According to the Compatibilist, when someone is deciding what to do and thinks to himself 'I can either choose to do this or to do that', what this means is 'If I prefer this, I shall choose this; if I prefer that, I shall choose that. And I *can* prefer either this or that, i.e. if I think there is more to be said in favour of this, I shall prefer this; if more in favour of that, then that,' and so on.

But should 'can' be interpreted in this 'hypothetical' way? Incompatibilists regularly insist that 'can' is 'categorical', *not* 'hypothetical'. 'Categorical' and 'hypothetical' are terms used by logicians. A hypothetical statement is one with an 'if' in it, like 'If it rains, it pours'. A categorical statement is one which is not 'iffy', like 'It is raining'. 'I can do' contains a hypothetical element, on the Compatibilist's view, because whether I actually do depends on the situation: 'if such and such, then I shall do; otherwise, not'.

The Incompatibilist objects that whether I can do something is a categorical fact about me, not something hypothetical. This, however, misunderstands the Compatibilist's position. The Compatibilist is not, or at least should not be, denying that whether I can do something is a categorical fact about me: if I *can* do something, then I actually categorically *can* do it; it is not that I can do it *if* some condition is fulfilled. An example will illustrate the point. I can swim; it is actually, categorically true that I can swim. At the same time this categorical fact contains a hypothetical element within it. For me to be able to swim I need not actually be swimming; but it must be true that if I am in water and want to swim, then I shall. But it does not follow that I can swim 'only hypothetically'. That would be the case if I can swim *only if* some condition is fulfilled. For instance, some children can swim *only if* they are wearing water wings. It is not (yet) true that they categorically can swim. But an experienced swimmer categorically can.

Unfortunately, Compatibilists have sometimes got confused over this issue (which is, admittedly, confusing). For instance, P.H. Nowell-Smith (in 1948), after examining a version of Argument *B*, commented:

> The fallacy in the argument lies in supposing that when we say 'A could have acted otherwise' we mean that A, *being what he was and being placed in the circumstances in which he was placed*, could have done something other than what he did. But in fact we never do mean this.

C.A. Campbell (in 1951) commented:

> What we really mean by the expression, he implies, is not a *categorical* but a *hypothetical* proposition. We mean 'A could have acted otherwise, *if he did not happen to be what he in fact was,* or *if he were placed in circumstances other than those in which he was in fact placed.*'

Campbell points out that 'A could have acted otherwise', so understood, is readily compatible with determinism, but has no bearing at all on whether A had free will. And Campbell is quite right. In asking whether A could have acted otherwise we are not interested in whether A with a different character or A in different circumstances could have acted differently. We are interested in whether A *himself* with the character he had and in *those* circumstances could have acted otherwise. What Nowell-Smith meant to say was that A himself with the character he actually had and in those circumstances could have acted otherwise because he *would* have (*not*: could have) acted otherwise if he had wanted to or if the situation had been different in some relevant respect.

In discussing Argument *B* I have talked a lot about the meanings of words, particularly the word 'can'. And you may be getting the impression that this discussion is just 'about words', as though it were not about anything *real*. But we are not in fact just talking about words. Philosophy is concerned with truth, not with anything merely verbal. But words are important. We can only describe reality by using words and we can only express and communicate our ideas by using words. In looking at words, our concern is not with the words, but with the reality they try to describe and the ideas they try to express.

are we autonomous? (second argument for premise (2) of argument A)

The argument we have just been looking at suggests that determinism rules out the existence of *alternative possibilities.* The argument we shall now consider suggests that determinism rules out *autonomy*. According to this argument, if our choices and actions are determined, then we are not the originators of our acts; we are no more creative than puppets or ventriloquists' dummies (though doubtless more complicated).

Robert Nozick (in 1981) proposed a way of formulating this argument in terms of the origination of value. He distinguished *originative value* from *contributory value*. The contributory value of something is the value it contributes, i.e. 'the value (amount) that wouldn't be there if it weren't'. Obviously we human beings have contributory value. But then so do lots of other things: 'a puppet can have contributory value also if in no other way could the children be brought to laugh so'. On Nozick's view, the truth of determinism is compatible with our having contributory value (puppets are presumably deterministic systems); but it is not compatible with our having originative value: originative value is *new* value brought into the world, value that was not simply predictable based on pre-existing conditions.

Using this idea of originative value (which we shall obviously have to examine), we can construct the following argument (*C*):

C (6) If we have free will, then we have originative value.

(7) If all our choices and actions are causally necessitated in accordance with deterministic laws, then it is not the case that we have originative value.

Therefore,

(2) If all our choices and actions are causally necessitated in accordance with deterministic laws, then we do not have free will.

Again, statement (2), which was a premise in Argument *A*, is the conclusion of this argument.

And again the Compatibilist will respond as she did to Argument *B*: either one (or both) of the premises is false or the words 'we have originative value' have a different meaning in premise (6) from their meaning in premise (7). Either way Argument *C* fails to prove its conclusion is true. The Compatibilist's main objection to Argument *C* is that it mistakenly suggests that, if our choices and acts are causally determined, we make no more contribution to the production of value than does a puppet. The puppet creates no new value because it is the puppet's operator who uses the puppet to create value. The puppet does not make choices or decide to act at all.

In replying to Argument *C*, the Compatibilist will claim that there is an important ambiguity in the idea of creating or originating new value. Nozick's definition of 'originative value' implies that new value is value which is not determined by antecedent causes; hence, obviously, the creation of new value in this sense is incompatible with determinism. The Compatibilist will say that free will does *not* imply the creation of new value in this sense. Rather, it implies a creation of a value which results entirely from the agent's choice and not from anything else. Even if the agent's choice is itself determined by antecedent causes, it is still true that the creation of value results entirely from the agent's choice – unless the agent's choice has been implanted in him by some other agent (as in post-hypnotic suggestion), in which case it is that other agent who has chosen to create the value. People decide to create a certain value; that is the originative value implied by free will. Since this sort of originative value is compatible with determinism, the originative value implied by free will (premise (6)) is not the originative value excluded by determinism (premise (7)).

Nozick writes:

> A daub of paint or a brushstroke in a painting may increase its aesthetic value, but that paint does not bring new value into the world; the value added in the placement of paint is added by the painter. Yet if he has no more autonomy than a paint blob, then although he is the vehicle through which value is added, and though his act of painting may be a component that is valuable, he does not originate any new value.

We can now see what, in the Compatibilist's view, is misleading about this. It is not true that, if the painter's acts are causally determined, then 'he has no more autonomy than a paint blob'. Nozick by his definition of 'originative value' is suggesting that if all our choices are causally determined, then we stand in the same relation to the causes of our choices as the paint blob does to the painter. But the only sense in which this is true is that our choices like the paint blob are causally determined (assuming the truth of determinism). This is not enough to prove that we are passive 'vehicles' (so long as we are not acting as a passive 'medium' for some other agent). We cannot validly argue (and Nozick would certainly not think that we can validly argue):

Paint blobs are caused.

Our choices are caused (assuming determinism).

Paint blobs are not autonomous.

Therefore, our choices are not autonomous.

This argument assumes that what is caused is not autonomous. But this cannot be assumed. It is what the Incompatibilist is trying to *prove*.

summary of discussion of argument C

Argument *C* contends that if we have free will then our acts must have originative, as well as contributory, value. Our acts have contributory value even if determinism is true. But contributory value is not enough.

The Incompatibilist claims that the originative value implied by free will is not compatible with determinism.

The Compatibilist claims that free will implies originative value in the sense that if we have free will we must be able to create value as a result of our own decision. But she claims that this sort of originative value is compatible with determinism. If originative value is defined in such a way that it is not compatible with determinism, then, says the Compatibilist, we need a further argument to show that this sort of originative value is implied by free will. In the Compatibilist's view 'originative value' must be interpreted in different ways if we want to make premises (6) and (7) both true. But in that case the argument is invalid because it commits a fallacy of equivocation.

is incompatibilism true?

We have now looked at two prominent arguments to support premise (2) of Argument *A*. And we have reached an impasse. The Compatibilist sees no reason to doubt that free will is compatible with determinism. The Incompatibilist is quite sure that if we understand free will correctly we shall see that free will and determinism cannot co-exist. It is hard to see how either party will convince the other.

In the debate between them the Compatibilist's aim is to show that the reasons why people have believed in Incompatibilism are not in fact good reasons, while the Incompatibilist's aim is to produce arguments like *B* and *C* to show that his view is correct. If the Incompatibilist in fact succeeded in doing this, that would of course end the matter. But even if the Incompatibilist has not yet succeeded, he may still do so. Similarly, however often the Compatibilist undermines the arguments in favour of Incompatibilism, that does not actually prove that Compatibilism is correct since a sound argument for Incompatibilism may lie in the future.

Perhaps the real problem lies in the notion of free will itself. Perhaps there is not just one idea of free will, but two (or more!).

the first reason reviewed

The Hard Determinist accepts Argument *A* as sound; its premises are true and the argument is valid. Can we resist the Hard Determinist's conclusion?

We have seen that there are two alternatives, depending on whether we accept premise (2) of Argument *A*. If we accept it, then we can resist the conclusion only by denying that determinism applies to our choices and actions. Someone who has been convinced by the arguments in support of premise (2) might think that our certainty about free will is greater than our certainty about determinism. Such a person might decide that on balance it is reasonable to reject premise (1) and thus resist the Hard Determinist's conclusion.

If, on the other hand, we reject premise (2), then, regardless of whatever we may think about determinism, Argument *A* fails.

Thus, if we wish to retain a belief in free will, we can either join with the Libertarians in rejecting premise (1) of Argument *A* or join with the Compatibilists in rejecting premise (2). Which should we do? Or should we accept both premises and agree with the Hard Determinist?

Many people find Libertarianism attractive. If Libertarianism is true, then we human beings with our free will are importantly different from other creatures and objects in the world. The clearest example of this is in Descartes' views. Descartes held that whereas everything else in the world is wholly physical, we have a non-physical mind which is exempt from deterministic laws; and that is how we have free will. Not all Libertarians go as far as Descartes, but all see beings with free will (i.e., principally, us) as importantly different in kind from the rest of the world around us.

Compatibilists, on the other hand, take a more naturalistic approach to human beings. They see us as literally part of nature; we differ from other things in the world only in degree of complexity and in the powers we have, particularly the powers of language-use and reasoning. There is a continuum between us and 'lower' creatures which do not have free will. If we look at animals from the simplest to the most complex, we observe new powers evolving with the growth in complexity. We do not believe that new powers evolve only if their possessors are exempt from scientific laws. On the contrary, it is the increase in complexity, together with the laws of nature, which explains the new powers. The power of having a free will is in this respect no different from the other powers (for example, perception, purposive behaviour) which we share with 'lower' creatures. Thus the Compatibilist sees no reason why determinism must remove free will. Some causes (for example, brainwashing) may remove free will, but causality as such (i.e. determinism) does not do so. If this is correct, then premise (2) of Argument *A* is false.

In opposition to this perspective, Hard Determinism and Libertarianism claim that the power of free will is one power which can never evolve according to naturalistic, deterministic principles. But while Hard Determinism says that we are wholly physical, deterministic beings and hence have no free will, Libertarianism says that we are in some sense not part of nature: we cannot be wholly understood in terms of deterministic principles (compare Kant). Libertarian views differ from each other in some important respects, but they all agree that in one way or another we *transcend* nature: either we are the causes of our actions and there is no antecedent cause which causes us to produce our actions (contrary to the deterministic principle that 'every event has a cause') or we as rational agents stand outside causality altogether and are subject only to the laws of reason.

The decision between Hard Determinism, Compatibilism, and Libertarianism is not simply a matter of looking at the various arguments and choosing which is most persuasive. It is a matter of one's whole view of human beings and our place in nature.

notes

Structure of logical argument. There are many introductory textbooks on the nature of logical argument. See, e.g., I. Copi, *Introduction to Logic*.

Hard Determinism. This view is not as popular with philosophers as the other two views (perhaps because philosophers like to think that they at least have free will). It has however been defended by Spinoza and Holbach (see chs. 2 and 3). It is also often assumed, without much argument, by psychologists and social scientists. See especially Skinner's *Science and Human Behaviour* and other writings by him. Contemporary philosophers defending Hard Determinism include John Hospers and Paul Edwards.

Soft Determinism. This view is very common among English-speaking philosophers and others who have been influenced by Hume's writings. Notable defenders include Hobbes and Hume (see ch. 2), J.S. Mill in the 19th century, and in this century, M. Schlick, R.E. Hobart, A.J. Ayer and P.H. Nowell-Smith.

Libertarianism. This view was held by Descartes, Kant, and Sartre (but takes a distinctive form in each of these writers, see ch. 2). In this century notable defenders include C.A. Campbell, R. Chisholm and P. van Inwagen.

Self-Determinism and Indeterminism. The claim that Libertarianism reduces all our choices to mere random chance (and hence in fact *denies* free will, paradoxically) is made at length by R.E. Hobart. For replies see Philippa Foot and C.A. Campbell.

Thomas Reid. 18th century Scottish philosopher, many of whose writings are critical of his contemporary, David Hume. The quotation is from ch. 9, Essay IV of his *Essays on the Active Powers of Man* (1768), which contains an interesting discussion of free will from a Libertarian perspective.

Compatibilism. For traditional defences of Compatibilism, see the writings of the Soft Determinists. However, as stated in the text, it is quite possible to defend Compatibilism without defending determinism; see, e.g., Kenny (quoted in ch. 8). For a defence of the view that determinism is compatible with 'The Varieties of Free Will Worth Wanting' see D.C. Dennett *Elbow Room*.

The principle 'If an agent can do X, and if doing X in the particular circumstances implies doing Y, then that agent can do Y'. The argument in the text derives from A. Kenny *Will, Freedom and Power,* pp. 155-7. He credits the discovery that this principle is fallacious to the medieval philosopher John Duns Scotus, from whom the argument about deceiving God is derived.

P.H. Nowell-Smith. 20th century British philosopher, defender of Compatibilism. The quotation is from his article 'Free Will and Moral Responsibility'.

C.A. Campbell. 20th century British philosopher, defender of Libertarianism. The quotation is from sec. V of his article 'Is "Free Will" a Pseudo-Problem?'

'Can': categorical or hypothetical? Some confusions about 'can' are discussed at length in a well-known article by J.L. Austin, 'Ifs and Cans'. For a discussion of Austin's views see R. Chisholm, 'J.L. Austin's Philosophical Papers' and P.H. Nowell-Smith 'Ifs and Cans'.

Robert Nozick. Contemporary American philosopher, defender of Libertarianism. The quotations are from his book *Philosophical Explanations* (1981), pp. 310-11 and 313.

5: seventeen more reasons for not believing in free will

In this chapter I shall look at seventeen more reasons for not believing that we have free will. Together with the First Reason, they are the principal considerations which have led people to doubt or deny that we have free will. I shall occasionally refer to my discussion in chapter 4, but no knowledge of what I said there is necessary in order to follow my discussions here. I do, though, presuppose knowledge of chapter 3, especially the section on determinism. It will turn out that many of the Reasons I shall be talking about seem to be based on the thesis of determinism.

A word of caution: it is probably not a good idea to read this chapter at one sitting. Like short stories, these Reasons are probably best taken one at a time.

second reason: fate

The Second Reason for not believing in free will is that all human actions are governed by Fate, and this fact means that we have no free will.

Fatalism is the view that the future is fixed in advance, so that nothing we may do can make any difference: there's only *one* way anything *can* turn out. If this is so, then free will is illusory. But do we have any reason to think that fatalism is true? St. Augustine links fatalism to astrology:

> But that all things come to pass by fate, we do not say; nay we affirm that nothing comes to pass by fate; for we demonstrate that the name of fate, as it is usually used by those who speak

61

of fate, meaning thereby the position of the stars at the time of each one's conception or birth, is an unmeaning word, for astrology itself is a delusion.

However, as I understand it, contemporary astrology says only that our stars have an influence on our lives, not that they fix our lives in detail. (I'm not prepared to contradict Augustine's claim that astrology is a delusion!)

The idea of Fate still survives in our so-called scientific age. When a longed for event fails to occur, people say 'It wasn't to be', as though some authority greater than us had decreed the event's non-occurrence. And Fate can be comforting; it implies that there is a pre-ordained pattern underlying the seemingly haphazard events of everyday life.

In myth and folklore Fate is a recurrent motif. Somerset Maugham captures the slightly creepy feeling that we get from thinking about Fate in this story:

DEATH SPEAKS

There was a merchant in Baghdad who sent his servant to market to buy provisions and in a little while the servant came back, white and trembling, and said, Master, just now when I was in the market-place I was jostled by a woman in the crowd and when I turned I saw it was Death that jostled me. She looked at me and made a threatening gesture; now, lend me your horse, and I will ride away from this city and avoid my fate. I will go to Samarra and there Death will not find me. The merchant lent him his horse, and the servant mounted it, and he dug his spurs in its flanks and as fast as the horse could gallop he went. Then the merchant went down to the market-place and he saw me standing in the crowd, and he came to me and said, Why did you make a threatening gesture to my servant when you saw him this morning? That was not a threatening gesture, I said, it was only a start of surprise. I was astonished to see him in Baghdad, for I had an appointment with him tonight in Samarra.

The idea that it is the very attempt to flee from Fate which starts the fateful ball rolling is familiar from the Oedipus myth. Oedipus was abandoned as an infant precisely to prevent the fulfilment of the prophecy that he would kill his father and marry his mother.

The trouble with Fate is that it is hard to find any actual evidence for the workings of its hidden hand. Such fatalistic-sounding remarks as 'Whatever will be will be' turn out on reflection just to be tautologies, no more informative than 'When it's raining, it's raining'. Certainly one can say 'It was fated' about everything which happens; the difficulty is to see what this adds to saying what happened.

More respectable, from a philosophical point of view, are (a) certain logical arguments which try to show that the future is fixed in advance, and (b) certain attempts to show that determinism implies a brand of fatalism.

(a) There are many arguments, from the simple-minded to the sophisticated, designed to show that the future is fixed, and thus that there is nothing we can do about it. Obviously, we cannot review every argument which tries to show this. But we can look at some. Here's the most simple-minded: Either I'm going to die tomorrow or I'm not. Suppose I'm going to die tomorrow. Then it *must* be the case that I'm going to die tomorrow. Therefore, there is nothing I can do to prevent my death tomorrow.

The question is, how did the 'must' get into the argument? Let us grant that it is a necessary truth (cannot be false) that either I'm going to die tomorrow or I'm not. It does *not* follow that whichever of these is the truth is necessarily true; that would be a logical fallacy.

Another argument is that if something is going to happen in the future then it was always true that it was going to happen. But if something was always true, then it was true before I was born. But I cannot alter anything that was true before I was born (the past is unchangeable). Therefore it is fixed that what will happen will happen, the future is as unchangeable as the past.

The question to be asked here is how a fact about the future (what *will* happen) can be turned into a fact about the past (it *was* always true that it would happen). Actually, and despite appearances, 'It was true before I was born that something (X) will happen tomorrow' is not a genuine statement about the past, because the fact which makes it true is a future fact (what will happen) not a past fact (what did happen). Hence it does not state something which was fixed before I was born.

There are other arguments of this sort. But the prospects for 'logical fatalism' are not good. How can one prove a substantive statement like 'fatalism is true' by purely logical means?

(b)   'Logical fatalism' may seem like a parlour-game for logicians. Arguments to show that determinism leads to fatalism are much more serious. If the arguments work, then we have further support for the First Reason; for if determinism implies fatalism and fatalism rules out free will then determinism rules out free will, just as the First Reason says. Consider this remark of Sir Arthur Eddington (in 1933):

> What significance is there in my mental struggle tonight whether I shall or shall not give up smoking, if the laws which govern the matter of the physical universe already pre-ordain for the morrow a configuration of matter consisting of pipe, tobacco, and smoke connected with my lips?

After quoting this remark, R.E. Hobart (a vigorous defender of both free will and determinism) wrote:

> No laws, according to determinism, pre-ordain such a configuration, unless I give up the struggle...Fatalism says that my morrow is determined no matter how I struggle. This is of course a superstition. Determinism says that my morrow is determined through my struggle.

Determinism says that future events will come about *because* of what we do. Fatalism says that future events will come about *in spite of* what we do.

Eddington's mistake is that he slides from the idea of determination, which is implicit in determinism, to the idea of *pre*-determination, which suggests fatalism. He uses the words 'already pre-ordain', as though the future course of events had already been settled *independently* of him. But this is not a correct statement of determinism. To quote Hobart again:

> The stream of causation runs through my deliberations and decision, and, if it did not run as it does run, the event would be different. The past cannot determine any event except through the present.

My future actions are not decided until I have decided them. It is thus a mistake to suppose that determinism implies fatalism.

We have now seen that fatalism can be arrived at in three ways: through superstitious belief, through purely logical arguments, and through determinism. The first of these is not a philosophical reason for believing anything. The second and third would be philosophically acceptable but the arguments are not compelling. Hence, for the time being at least, we may reject fatalism.

third reason: inevitability

It is inevitable that the future will unfold in a certain way. We do not have free will in regard to what is inevitable. So we do not have free will.

There is an obvious link between the Second and Third Reasons. Fatalism implies that future events are inevitable. But it is possible to argue for inevitability without arguing for Fate. Some things are certainly inevitable, for instance, death. We are not free to avoid dying (at least not altogether). Is everything that happens inevitable?

Certainly the future does not *appear* inevitable, apart from some certainties like death. But this may be due to our ignorance. From our standpoint in the present the past is rigid and unchangeable while the future is fluid and changeable. But this may be an illusion of perspective. Consider weather forecasts. The forecaster confidently predicts that the sun will shine tomorrow. When it does not, he just as confidently explains why it rained. It now appears that the rain was inevitable, and only our ignorance prevented us from realizing it was. Perhaps everything in the future is like this. We all agree that the past is unchangeable; perhaps the future is too. As D.C. Dennett has written,

> It is often said that no one can change the past. This is true enough, but it is seldom added that no one can change the future either. If the past is unchangeable, the future is unavoidable – on anyone's account. The future consists, timelessly, of the sequence of events that will happen, whether determined to happen or not, and it makes no more sense to speak of

avoiding those events than it does to speak of avoiding the events that have already happened.

Now, obviously no one can make what will happen *also* not happen. That would be self-contradictory, like eating your cake and still having it. But does that make the future unavoidable? Even if in fact I will take the day off tomorrow, that does not mean that I cannot work tomorrow, only that I will not. But if I can work tomorrow, then it is not (is it?) inevitable that I shall take the day off tomorrow.

Why do we distinguish the unchangeable past from the fickle future? The commonsense answer is that by our actions we can causally affect the future but not the past. Whatever I do now, the past will remain as it is. But not so with the future (unless fatalism is true). The future is not inevitable; it is not going to be the same whatever I do now. Some things will be the same whatever we do: these are inevitable.

Armed with this idea of the inevitable, we are in a good position to distinguish what is inevitable from what isn't. If I jump out of a high window without a parachute, rope or other means of support, it is inevitable that I will fall. That is to say, whatever I may try to do about it, I shall fall. Inevitable happenings are outside our control (see chapter 3). But it is not inevitable that I will do everything which I will in fact do. Hence it seems that I still have free will in regard to very many things (though not everything).

Inevitability excludes free will, since we do not have the freedom to avoid what cannot be avoided. Consequently many people who believe in free will have denied the doctrine of *historical inevitability* (the doctrine that future history will inevitably take a certain course) on the ground that it denies free will. Thus Dennett, for instance, talks about 'the pernicious idea of historical inevitability'.

Certainly the idea of historical inevitability is pernicious if it means that people should just sit around waiting for things to happen, instead of trying to determine their outcome. And it is frightening that some people should believe that a nuclear

holocaust is inevitable, as though there were nothing that anyone could do about it. But it does not follow from this that the idea of historical inevitability is intrinsically incorrect or that it altogether excludes our having free will.

I believe the essential idea of historical inevitability (as this notion is employed by Marxists, for example) is that whatever any particular individual may decide to do, history will nevertheless follow a certain path. The idea is not that the future is independent of what we all do – as though society might undergo certain changes, although nobody actually did anything. Rather, the idea is that whatever any particular individual may decide to do, there will still be other individuals who will act in such a way as to bring about a certain result.

According to this idea of historical inevitability, we might still have free will. It might still be the case that each individual freely decides what to do. But the inevitable result (unavoidable by any particular individual) of all these particular individual decisions taken together is that future history follows one course rather than another. This does not, of course, provide a defence of historical inevitability in itself, but only a defence against the claim that it rules out free will and hence can be dismissed on the ground that we do have free will.

We have not yet discerned any inevitability about the future which rules out our having free will. There is one further argument, however, namely determinism again. It is argued that if determinism is true of our choices and actions, then we can only choose to do one thing, we cannot choose to do anything else, hence it is inevitable that we choose as we do, and therefore we have no free will. Consider the following, from Skinner's *Walden Two:*

> Linguistically or logically there seem to be two possibilities, but I submit that there's only one in fact. The determining forces may be subtle but they are inexorable...It was all lawful. You had no choice.

The crucial move in this argument is that the 'determining forces' make a certain choice 'inexorable' because we cannot choose to do otherwise than we do do. I have discussed this claim at length in chapter 4.

fourth reason: predictability
Human behaviour is predictable, just as the movements of the planets are. Hence we have no more free will than do the planets.

It is true that sometimes when someone correctly predicts what we are going to do, this makes us think of ourselves as somewhat dull and robot-like members of the human species. But this is far from always being the case. R.E. Hobart puts the point well:

> If you are to be alone in a room with £1000 belonging to another on the table and can pocket it without anyone knowing the fact, and if I predict that you will surely *not* pocket it, that is not an insult...On the other hand, there are cases where prediction is really disparaging. If I say when you make a remark, "I knew you were going to say that", the impression is not agreeable.

> My exclamation seems to say that your mind is so small and
> simple that one can predict its ideas.

The belief that it is inferior to be predictable appears to place a
certain superior value on being unpredictable. But it is unpredictability as manifesting interesting complexity, not unpredictability in itself, which confers this superior value.

Historically, the Fourth Reason for not believing in free will
was first debated in connection with God's foreknowledge of all
our choices and actions. It was supposed that if God foreknows
all that we will do, then we *must* do it and therefore have no
free will. Predictability, in the form of divine foreknowledge, is
thus thought to lead to a sort of fatalism. This view was
forcefully denounced by St. Augustine:

> Now, against the sacrilegious and impious darings of reason,
> we assert both that God knows all things before they come to
> pass, and that we do by our free will whatsoever we know and
> feel to be done by us only because we will it.

Augustine's argument to reconcile our free will with God's
foreknowledge rests on a distinction between two sorts of
necessity. Freedom is often contrasted with necessity (as we
saw in chapter 2), but Augustine holds that not all necessity
reduces or takes away our freedom. The necessity which takes
away our freedom is the necessity which reduces our *power:*

> If we call *our necessity* that which is not in our power but, even
> though we be unwilling, effects what it can effect – as, for
> instance, the necessity of death –, it is manifest that our wills
> by which we live uprightly or wickedly are not under any such
> necessity. For we do many things which, if we were not willing,
> we certainly would not do.

There is another sort of necessity which does not reduce
one's power. Augustine illustrates this sort of necessity by
considering God's nature and powers:

> We do not put the life of God or the foreknowledge of God under
> necessity [of the first sort] if we should say that it is necessary
> that God should live forever and foreknow all things. His power
> is not diminished when we say that He cannot die or fall into
> error. For the impossibility of this is such that, if it were
> possible, He would be of *less* power.

Now we must ask, if it is necessary that we act as God foreknows, does this limit our powers or not? According to Augustine it does not:

> It is not the case, therefore, that because God foreknew what would be in the power of our wills, there is for that reason nothing in the power of our wills.

God's foreknowledge does not limit our powers because it does not *affect* them in any way: 'A man does not sin *because* God foreknew that he would sin.'

In modern times predictability is associated with determinism. As Pierre de Laplace wrote in the 19th century:

> We ought then to regard the present state of the universe as the effect of its antecedent state and the cause of the state that is to follow. An intelligence knowing, at a given instant of time, all things of which the universe consists, would be able to comprehend the movements of the largest bodies in the universe and those of the lightest atoms in one single formula, provided his intellect were sufficiently powerful to subject all data to analysis. To him nothing would be uncertain; both past and future would be present to his eyes.

However, even avid determinists like Skinner disavow predictability as a realistic goal. As his character Frazier says in *Walden Two:*

> I didn't say that behaviour is always predictable, any more than the weather is always predictable. There are often too many factors to be taken into account. We can't measure them all accurately, and we couldn't perform the mathematical operations needed to make a prediction if we had the measurements.

Determinism is thought to imply predictability *in principle* (as opposed to practice) because if a cause or set of causes sufficient to bring about a certain effect exists and is known to exist, then one can predict the effect. But it is a mistake to think that unpredictability disproves determinism. Determinism is a thesis about the relations between events in nature, not a thesis about predictability.

Planetary motions are predictable because they are readily observable, and there are no unknown or unpredictable interfering factors which would upset our predictions. But human beings are obviously not like that. So to argue that human beings do not have free will because planets do not is to use a false, or at least unsubstantiated, analogy.

In summary, we may say that the Fourth Reason adds nothing to the First. Either it is simply a re-statement of the First Reason with 'predictable' substituted for 'determined', or it rests on the claim that what is predictable is simple and therefore lacking in free will – in which case we need a further argument to show that we are predictable in this sense.

fifth reason: mechanism

Machines do what they are designed to do, they do not have free will. We are machines. So we do not have free will.

If we consider familiar everyday machines like washing machines, record players, even chess-playing computers, then it does seem that being a machine is hardly conducive to having free will. But are we machines like that? If we define the word 'machine' in such a way that we would count as machines, then it becomes problematic whether all machines lack free will.

The Fifth Reason for not believing in free will would be just plain wrong, not merely problematic, if Descartes' views are correct. According to Descartes we are certainly not machines of any sort. Our bodies are mechanical systems, but our minds are not. Descartes argues that, whereas we human beings act 'from knowledge' and our 'reason is a universal instrument that may serve in all kinds of circumstances', machines act only in virtue of the arrangement of their working parts and 'it is morally [i.e. in practice] impossible that a machine should contain so many varied arrangements as to act in all events of life in the way reason enables us to act'. Of course, in the 17th century electronics had not even been thought of. But Descartes would still have a good argument if we have *infinite* mental capacity; for it is hard to see how a mechanism could have infinite capacity: mechanisms are by definition *finite*.

But do we have infinite mental capacity? The human minds we know about can indeed switch from one subject (science) to another (philosophy), to another (mathematics), to another (chess), to another (bee-keeping). But we do not know of any mind which can embrace within itself *all* forms of knowledge. Part of the reason we write things down is that we can't keep all of them 'in mind'. So perhaps what we should say is, not that our minds are infinite (= everything included), but only that they are indefinite (= nothing excluded). Now there is nothing to prevent a machine from having an indefinite capacity too. So it seems we have no built-in advantage, in respect of capacity, over all possible future machines.

The Fifth Reason sets up a contrast between 'being designed' and 'having free will'. But are these mutually exclusive? The contrast comes about because we compare a human being 'of his own free will' *deciding* to do something in a certain situation and, on the other hand, a machine *designed* to do automatically exactly the same thing in the same situation. For instance, a well-designed chess-playing computer will make exactly the same move as a human being of comparable skill will decide to make 'of his own free will'. The *design* is precisely intended to duplicate the *decision*. But this situation, of design replacing decision, may not be the only possibility. It is conceivable that a mechanism might be designed so as to be capable of making genuine decisions. Or if it is not conceivable we need a further argument (perhaps the next Reason) to show why not. It is hard to see how design by itself excludes free will since many people think that we are designed by a creator in such a way as to have free will.

The problem for the Fifth Reason is this: unless we agree with Descartes, our evidence that machines must lack free will comes from machines markedly inferior to ourselves, and our evidence that *we* are machines depends on the possibility of constructing a mechanical theory of human beings, but the more likely it becomes that we can construct such a theory, the less likely it becomes that being a machine necessarily excludes having free will.

It may be objected, on behalf of the Fifth Reason, that if we were created by an intelligent (non-human) being then we have no reason to think that we have free will any more than the chess-playing computers do which we have created. Perhaps we are playthings of the gods, toys designed to think we have free will when we don't! This is conceivable, in the same way that it is conceivable that the world does not exist when no one is observing it or that we are all brains in a vat fooled into thinking we have human bodies. These are standard philosophical fantasies and they have a valid role to play in deciding when (or indeed whether) our claims to know things are (ever) justified. But this fantasy is to be distinguished from the idea that we are mechanisms. Even if in the fantasized situation we have no free will (and I agree we wouldn't), it does not follow that in the actual world we have no free will because we are mechanisms.

sixth reason: programming
We have been programmed since birth (perhaps even before) to think and act as we do. Therefore we have no free will.

It is a common view that society, through parents, teachers, and so on, 'programmes' us to behave as we do. Computers are programmed to carry out their tasks. Unless they malfunction, everything they do is in accordance with their programmes, though not necessarily *prescribed* by their programmes: some programmes allow certain 'randomizing', i.e. not explicitly prescribed, procedures. Computers have no free will, so there is no reason to say we do either.

The question that needs to be raised about this argument is: are we or are we not able to resist our programming and act contrary to it?

If we *can* act contrary to the 'programming' (whether or not we do in fact act contrary to it), and if this would not constitute a 'malfunction', then the influences (education, religious indoctrination, whatever) that we are acting against cannot literally be regarded as programming.

If we *cannot* act contrary to the 'programming', then why can't we? It is said that some religious or quasi-religious sects or cults do literally programme their initiates. Through sleep-deprivation, enforced lack of privacy, rhythmic chanting, and other endearing practices, they break down a person's mind so that he or she is captive to the organization. If this is the case, then such a person may indeed be viewed as 'programmed' and may indeed lose all freedom of will. 'Treating' or 'curing' someone who has gone through this process is sometimes called 'deprogramming' (though this may well just be a pretentious pseudo-scientific label).

It would of course be a mistake to argue that just because those people are programmed, we all are. Someone who says that we are all programmed because no one can choose or act otherwise than she or he does is repeating the First Reason, not producing a new Reason (unless some further argument is forthcoming).

Thus it is quite unclear whether and, if so, in what sense we are 'programmed'. But supposing we are, does being programmed necessarily exclude having free will? No doubt some forms of programming exclude free will, but do all?

Suppose, for instance, that we have one or more 'high-level' programmes built into us which can initiate, modify, or even eliminate certain 'lower-level' programmes. There is thus a hierarchy of programmes inside us (in our brains): the higher the level of a programme the more sub-programmes there are below it, i.e. subject to modification by it. I am not for one moment suggesting that this is the case (I have no idea). But supposing it were, would the fact that inside us there is a 'highest level' programme, i.e. one with none higher, imply that we have no free will? Once the question is put like this I think it becomes evident that the impulse to respond 'Of course it would' is the result of thinking of rather simple programmes.

The mathematician Alan Turing in a classic article on this subject (1950) refers to a Lady Lovelace who maintained that machines only do what they are told to, hence have no free will. This is certainly true of rather 'low level' machines with 'low level' programmes. But what about a machine with a 'highest possible level' programme? I find I have no intuitions whatever about a machine with such a programme. (I'm assuming that everything which is programmed is in some sense a machine; in this Reason I'm interested in the programming, not in whether it's a machine.) If my intuitions are correct, it is an open question whether programming necessarily excludes free

will. It is also an unresolved question whether we are programmed.

We thus arrive at the same conclusion about the Sixth
Reason as about the Fifth (with 'programmed' substituted for
'machine').

seventh reason: character

Our actions come from our characters. We do not make our
characters. Hence we have no free will.

John Stuart Mill in the 19th century called this the doctrine
of 'Modified Fatalism', which he contrasted both with 'Pure
Fatalism' and with 'Causation' (i.e. determinism):

> Pure, or Asiatic Fatalism – the fatalism of the Oedipus – holds
> that our actions do not depend upon our desires...The other
> kind, Modified Fatalism I will call it, holds that our actions are
> determined by our will, our will by our desires, and our desires
> by the joint influence of the motives presented to us and of our
> individual character; but that, our character having been made
> for us and not by us, we are not responsible for it, nor for the
> actions it leads to, and should in vain attempt to alter them.
> The true doctrine of the Causation of human actions maintains,
> in opposition to both, that not only our conduct, but our
> character, is in part amenable to our will; that we can, by
> employing the proper means, improve our character; and that
> if our character is such that while it remains what it is, it
> necessitates us to do wrong, it will be just to apply motives
> which will necessitate us to strive for its improvement, and so
> emancipate ourselves from the other necessity.

But where do these 'motives' come from? The Modified Fatalist
will object that they are as much part of our character as the
rest of it. Consequently, to accept Causation is to accept
Modified Fatalism.

In opposition to Modified Fatalism, Aristotle maintained that
people are responsible for their characters (see chapter 2).
Aristotle insists that we are not born with our character, nor is
our character implanted in us by external forces. Rather, we
acquire a certain character through acting in a certain way.
Since our actions are 'voluntary' and 'up to us', so our characters
must be voluntary too. Even if our character becomes so

ingrained that we cannot alter it, still there was always a time when it was in our power to do so:

> Only an utterly senseless person can fail to know that our characters are the result of our behaviour; and if a man knowingly acts in a way that will result in his becoming wicked, he must be said to be wicked voluntarily. Again, it is unreasonable to say that a man who acts wickedly does not wish to be wicked or a man who acts self-indulgently does not wish to be self-indulgent, though it by no means follows that he can stop being wicked and become good merely by wishing to do so.

But the Modified Fatalist is likely to be unimpressed by these considerations. For where do the person's actions come from before he acquires a wicked or self-indulgent character? They must come from some earlier character, and thus the Seventh Reason still applies. Consider Paul Edwards' defence of the Seventh Reason (in 1957):

> Let us suppose that both A and B are compulsive and suffer intensely from their neuroses. Let us assume that there is a therapy that could help them, which could materially change their character structure, but that it takes a great deal of energy and courage to undertake the treatment. Let us suppose that A has the necessary energy and courage while B lacks it. A undergoes the therapy and changes in the desired way. B just gets more and more compulsive and more and more miserable. Now, it is true that A helped form his own later character. But his starting point, his desire to change, his energy and courage, were already there. They may or may not have been the result of previous efforts on his own part. But there must have been a first effort, and the effort at that time was the result of factors that were not of his making.

Edwards believes that 'a person's character is ultimately the product of factors over which he had no control' and that only someone who 'originally chose his own character' would have free will.

In direct opposition to Edwards' views are R.E. Hobart's. Hobart considers it bizarre to hold that because we didn't choose our own characters we lack free will. He maintains

(a) that a free act is an act which comes from one's *self*,

(b) that one's self *is* one's character,

(c) that to praise or blame someone is to ascribe a certain character (good or bad) to that person:

> A man is to be blamed only for what he does himself, for that alone tells what he is. He did not make his character; no, but he made his acts. Nobody blames him for making such a character, but only for making such acts. And to blame him for that is simply to say that he is a bad act-maker...To cause his original self a man must have existed before his original self. Is there something humiliating to him in the fact that he is not a contradiction in terms? If there were a being who made his 'original character', and made a fine one, and we proceeded to praise him for it, our language would turn out to be a warm ascription to him of a still earlier character, so that the other would not have been original at all. To be praised or blamed you have to be; and be a particular person; and the praise or blame is telling what kind of person you are. There is no other meaning to be extracted from it. Of course, a man does exist before his later self, and in that other sense he can be a moral *causa sui* [cause of himself]...It is fantastic to say that he finds his character on his hands. It is nothing but the moral description of himself. It is that self alone that wields his hands.

Hobart, unlike Edwards, thinks that the question of where our character comes from is unimportant. But it is not unimportant. If someone's character were forcibly implanted in her or were the result of childhood experience too ghastly to recount, then we might indeed want to say that such a person lacked free will.

All three of Hobart's statements (a - c) are open to objection. First, it is not sufficient for freedom that an act comes from one's self; one's self must also be free. Second, one's self is not the same thing as one's character: everyone, or almost everyone, at some point does something which is not 'in character'. To say that it is not *their* act because it does not express their character is strange. Third, to praise or blame someone is not necessarily to ascribe a good or bad character to that person. Hobart writes, 'All self-reproach is self-judging, and all judging is imputing a character'. But when I reproach myself for being unjust I am criticising my act, not my character. I am saying that this act is *not* representative of my character (as I would like it to be, at least). Of course one *can* criticize one's character. But it is incorrect to say that all self-reproach is 'imputing a character'. It is incorrect in another way too: it implies that everyone who has a bad character is liable to be blamed. But if, for instance, someone is insane (through no fault of his own) and as a result of his insanity has a violent character, we would *not* blame him, at least not if we were being fair.

Mill made a similar mistake to Hobart's when he discussed punishment and 'fault'. In reply to the argument that criminals should not be punished because it is not their 'fault' that they enter on a life of crime, Mill replies that no criminal will feel that his act 'was not his own fault':

> For, first, it was at all events his own defect or infirmity, for which the expectation of punishment is the appropriate cure. And secondly, the word fault, so far from being inapplicable, is the specific name for the kind of defect or infirmity which he has displayed – insufficient love of good and aversion to evil.

But this is merely a play on words. Mill has passed from 'fault', in the sense of 'what a person can justly be held responsible for', to 'fault' in the quite different Hobartian sense of 'a kind of defect or infirmity', in this case 'insufficient love of good and aversion to evil'. To say that it is automatically a person's fault (in the first sense) if he or she displays a fault (in the second sense) is quite unwarranted.

Must we conclude that the Seventh Reason is valid? I think not. We can find enough in the writings of Aristotle, Mill and Hobart to rebut it.

First, even if, as Edwards argues, our character is 'ultimately' out of our control, since we had no control over its initial formation, it does not follow that it is *now* out of our control. (To some extent Edwards is following Holbach's argument which I examined in chapter 3.) Second, by arguing that everything we do to improve our character is itself a manifestation of our character, Edwards has not shown that we have no control over our character; all he has shown is that we *do* in fact improve our character only if we are a certain sort of person. To show that only a certain sort of person *can* improve his character, Edwards would have to show that we cannot do what we do not do. But to show this Edwards would have to go back to the First Reason and argue that if determinism is true then we cannot act otherwise than we do. For the fact (if it is one) that all our actions express our character does not imply that we *cannot* act contrary to our character, but only that we do not.

This is not to deny that, as I have already suggested, there could be cases where people in fact cannot act contrary to their character or where their character is the result of such un- believable circumstances that it is quite unreasonable to expect them to behave differently from the way they do. In such cases, we should be prepared to admit that a person's freedom of will is limited. It is plausible to say, for example, that the klepto- maniac steals because that is the way he is: 'Whatever he resolved to do, he would steal all the same', as A.J. Ayer says. It would thus appear that he lacks the free will to act differently. But these special cases in no way show the general validity of the Seventh Reason.

eighth reason: environment
Our behaviour is not under the control of ourselves but of the environment. Hence we do not have free will.

The psychologist B.F. Skinner is well known for his insist- ence, in a long series of publications over a period of fifty years or more, on the environment's control of our behaviour. In Skinner's view the belief in free will is the belief that to explain behaviour we should look inside our heads at the exploits of a 'little person' (*homunculus* in Latin) who controls our behav- iour, whereas in fact we should look at the environment. Things do go on in our heads, of course, but Skinner deems them unimportant for the psychological explanation of behaviour:

> The objection to inner states is not that they do not exist, but that they are not relevant in a functional [i.e. causal] analysis. We cannot account for the behaviour of any system while staying wholly inside it; eventually we must turn to forces operating upon the organism from without.

If determinism is correct (and Skinner is sure that it is), then our 'inner states' must be the effects of external events ('stimuli') and the causes of behaviour ('responses'). We can therefore omit the inner states and talk only about stimulus and response.

In a sense this is indeed possible. If *A* causes *B* and *B* causes *C*, we may abbreviate the causal chain and say simply that *A* causes *C*. But of course we must not infer that *B* plays no role in the causation of *C*. On the contrary, it is only *because A* causes *B* and *B* causes *C* that *A* causes *C*. Skinner has a bad habit of talking as if the external factor (*A*) is the real cause, not anything inner (*B*): 'the environment builds the basic repertoire with which we keep our balance, walk, play games, handle instruments and tools, talk, write, sail a boat, drive a car, or fly a plane.' But obviously all causes are equally real, whether they are external or internal.

In fact, on Skinner's own view, the environment no more controls us than we control it. This is simply determinism (everything is caught up in the web of causation). But if so then the Eighth Reason adds nothing to the First. Skinner likes to give the impression that the environment is in a pre-eminent position. But this is true only in the sense that, as D.C. Dennett puts it, there is 'a benign tendency of the selecting environment, over the evolutionary long run, to design creatures that have *in themselves* a benign tendency to make the right discriminations – for themselves':

> The environment is not designed to *tell* us what to do; we are designed to *figure out* from the indifferent environment what to do. So it is unwise, even in the light of this indirect but systematically helpful tendency over the long run, to speak of the environment controlling us.

Skinner himself realizes that there are many different forms of 'environmental control':

> The extent to which we commend someone for operating a complex piece of equipment depends on the circumstances. If it is obvious that he is simply imitating another operator, that someone is 'showing him what to do', we give him very little credit – at most only for being able to imitate and execute the behaviour. If he is following oral instructions, if someone is 'telling him what to do', we give him slightly more credit – at

least for understanding the language well enough to follow directions. If he is following written instructions, we give him additional credit for knowing how to read. But we give him credit for 'knowing how to operate the equipment' only if he does so without current direction, though he may have learned through imitation or by following oral or written instructions. We give him maximal credit if he has discovered how to operate it without help, since he then owes nothing to any instructor at any time; his behaviour has been shaped wholly by the relatively inconspicuous contingencies arranged by the equipment, and these are now past history.

Skinner is arguing that there is an 'inverse relationship between credit and the conspicuousness of causes'. It seems not to occur to him that the reason why the last person gets 'maximal credit' is that he has had to think more than the others have. If all these different situations are equally cases of 'environmental control', distinguishable only by the conspicuousness of the causes, then there is nothing in this notion which can reduce our freedom beyond what is implied by the thesis of determinism (First Reason).

Of course sometimes we *are* dominated by the environment, e.g. if we are being swept along by a tidal wave or an avalanche our freedom to act otherwise is, to say the least, seriously impaired. But it is fallacious to argue that because the environment sometimes takes away our freedom therefore it always does.

ninth reason: heredity
We are controlled by our genes. Hence we have no free will.

Genetic determinism, the thesis that our behaviour is under the control of our genes, seems to exclude free will since we obviously have no control over our genes. In recent years, ethology, the science of animal behaviour, and sociobiology, the science of the genetic bases of social behaviour, have made genetic determinism appear more plausible.

Richard Dawkins, in his book *The Selfish Gene* (1976), writes:

> We are survival machines – robot vehicles blindly programmed to preserve the selfish molecules known as genes.

In what way are our genes supposed to be selfish?

> The argument of this book is that we, and all other animals, are machines created by our genes. Like successful Chicago gangsters, our genes have survived in some cases for millions of years, in a highly competitive world. This entitles us to expect certain qualities in our genes. I shall argue that a predominant quality to be expected in a successful gene is ruthless selfishness. This gene selfishness will usually give rise to selfishness in individual behaviour. However, as we shall see, there are special circumstances in which a gene can achieve its own selfish goals best by fostering a limited form of altruism at the level of individual animals. 'Special' and 'limited' are important words in the last sentence. Much as we might wish to believe otherwise, universal love and the welfare of the species as a whole are concepts which simply do not make evolutionary sense.

It would seem from this that we are helplessly in the grip of our genes, which are bent only on replicating themselves unto eternity. But Dawkins seems to think we can outwit our genes:

> My own feeling is that a human society based simply on the gene's law of universal ruthless selfishness would be a very nasty society in which to live. But unfortunately, however much we may deplore something, it does not stop it being true...Be warned that if you wish, as I do, to build a society in which individuals co-operate generously and unselfishly towards a common good, you can expect little help from biological nature. Let us try to *teach* generosity and altruism, because we are born selfish.

We are not powerless against our genes:

> We have the power to defy the selfish genes of our birth...We can even discuss ways of deliberately cultivating and nurturing pure, disinterested altruism – something that has no place in nature, something that had never existed before in the whole history of the world. We are built as gene machines...,but we have the power to turn against our creators. We, alone on Earth, can rebel against the tyranny of the selfish replicators.

In saying this Dawkins must be rejecting genetic determinism, for otherwise he would be contradicting himself. He is saying that although our genes influence our behaviour and, left to their own devices, would completely control it, we can intervene to prevent genetic influences which run counter to cherished social ideals. So we might simply conclude that Dawkins has given us no reason to accept the Ninth Reason, and pass on. However, his remarks are, I believe, very misleading. Contrary to what he suggests, there is no intrinsic antagonism between 'us' with our social ideals and 'our selfish genes'.

When Dawkins says that 'universal love and the welfare of the species as a whole are concepts which simply do not make evolutionary sense' and that 'pure, disinterested' altruism 'has no place in nature', he cannot be saying that universal love, etc., are *excluded* by the fact that we are naturally evolved creatures; for if he were, why would he hold out the hope of realizing these ideals? But at the same time he must see some tension between universal love, etc., and our genetic nature; for why else should he say that we 'can expect little help from biological nature', and that to build a genuinely altruistic society would be to *rebel* against the tyranny of the selfish replicators'?

Dawkins seems to have slid from the statement, 'Evolution (natural selection) by itself would never produce a society based on pure, disinterested altruism', to the quite different statement, 'A society based on pure, disinterested altruism is contrary to evolution'. But evolution need not be opposed to what evolution by itself will never produce.

Perhaps Dawkins has been misled by his statement that we are 'blindly programmed to preserve' our genes and that we are 'machines created by our genes'. The former is true in the sense that we are genetically programmed so as to preserve our genes (for if we were not, how would they have survived this far?), and that the latter is true in the sense that our genes provide a sort of 'blueprint' for our 'construction'. But it is easy to pass from these biological facts to the questionable, and unscientific, conclusion that our genes have told us how to behave and that they will not be co-operative if we decide to behave differently.

If we human beings are purely physical, then our inherited equipment includes our reason. Now it is no doubt true that we are going beyond our genetic programming when by the use of our reason we decide to establish a genuinely co-operative society. But in doing so we are not *rebelling* against our genes. Our genes will have as good a chance, if not better, of surviving in a co-operative society as in a competitive one.

Dawkins' most puzzling assertion is that 'a human society based simply on the gene's law of universal ruthless selfishness would be a very nasty society'. What does he mean by a society 'based' on the gene's law? He might mean 'a society in which everyone behaved as if he or she were a selfish gene' or he might mean 'a society as evolved solely by natural selection and without any culture or non-genetically-based institutions'. The latter society would not be 'human' in any recognizable sense; but in so far as it is possible, why should it be any more 'nasty' than bee or ant societies, which seem quite pleasant, if exhausting? The former idea is hard to make sense of because genes do not have social relations comparable to those between humans. Dawkins seems to have been taken in by his comparison between genes and Chicago gangsters. In any case, why should observations about such a society be relevant to our actual society?

Dawkins' errors (as I take them to be) are not biological errors; they consist of faulty inferences from biological facts about evolution, genes, and natural selection. Unfortunately, when scientists make unwarranted inferences from scientific subject-matter, they lend the prestige of science (and, often, of their own scientific accomplishments) to these inferences, which are then treated as 'scientific' and as worthy of credence as the genuinely scientific (one hopes) considerations on which they are based.

In his book *On Human Nature* (1978), E.O. Wilson seems to be suggesting that if a form of behaviour is found in all human societies it is likely to be genetically based. But this is speculation, not a scientific discovery. Wilson proceeds to look around for a genetic explanation of homosexuality, although there is no evidence that it is genetically based. Homosexuality may pose a theoretical problem for sociobiology (since homosexuals are presumably less likely to transmit their genes to the next generation), but it does not pose a *real* problem for sociobiology unless it is inherited.

On the basis of studies of animal behaviour and comparisons with human behaviour, ethologists have argued that we possess instincts which are genetically based. For example: ethologists have found evidence of innate inclinations to aggressive behaviour in certain animals. Human beings have killed an incredible number of human beings. Therefore, it is concluded, human beings have an aggressive instinct.

Konrad Lorenz in his book *On Aggression* (1963) and other writings has claimed that human beings need periodically to 'let off steam'. After a period of peaceful co-existence with our fellow human we are, he says, more likely to be provoked to anger even by small incidents, a phenomenon he calls 'threshold-lowering':

> The 'polar malady' which emerges among members of expeditions, the crew of small boats, and so on, is nothing less than massive threshold-lowering of the behaviour patterns of angry outbreaks. Anybody who has become acquainted with this knows how minor irritations can eventually have a ridiculously angering effect. Even when one has full insight into one's own response, one is unable to prevent oneself from boiling with rage at certain small characteristics of a companion, for example, a cough or a peculiar way of speaking. In so responding to a friend, one behaves fundamentally just like the male of an isolated Cichlid fish pair which will finally attack and kill the female following the absence of threatening conspecifics to chase away from the family. This response pattern is particularly typical of *Geophagus*, and one can prevent this by placing a mirror in the aquarium for the male to abreact [i.e. discharge] his aggression.

The word 'abreact', which comes from psychoanalysis, is used here to suggest that aggression wells up inside poor *Geophagus* to the point where it has to be discharged. But the evidence actually indicates only that this fish is so programmed to repel 'invaders' that it will even attack its mate. Lorenz associates human aggression with an emotional reaction, anger, but it would be far-fetched to say that *Geophagus* is angry. Thus it is unclear why Lorenz says that the aggressive human 'behaves fundamentally just like' the aggressive fish.

Let us, however, concede (for the sake of argument) that human beings have some innate aggressive tendencies. Does this fact explain human destructiveness? Not at all, not even on Lorenz' own account. As Lorenz is at pains to point out, aggressive instinct in lower animals comes complete with built-in inhibitions. If the human species is in danger, it is not from our instincts but from our *lack* of genetic programming:

> The price which man had to pay for his constitutive liberty in thinking processes and behavioural acts is that of adaptedness to a specific environment and a specific form of social existence, which in all sub-human organisms is guaranteed by species-specific, inherited action and response norms.

In particular, we have no built-in mechanism to safeguard against the use of weapons:

> The failure of killing inhibitions in the situation produced by the invention of weapons is principally based on the fact that the innate mechanisms releasing an inhibition do not respond in the new situation...The firing of a long-range gun or the dropping of a bomb is so thoroughly 'impersonal' that normal human beings who are absolutely incapable of throttling a mortal enemy with their hands are nevertheless able, without further ado, to apply finger-pressure to deliver up thousands of women and children to a horrible death.

The solution, then, is obvious: educate our reason and emotion so as to provide a cultural inhibition on destructiveness to replace the built-in inhibitions we do not have.

Lorenz suggests that our failure to use our reason to prevent human destructiveness shows 'blockage of the application of rational thought by innate, species-specific action and response patterns'. He bases his opinion on the view that 'even some-body of sub-normal intelligence can immediately see what would have to happen, and what must be avoided, in order to prevent the self-destruction of mankind'. This is an incredibly simplistic view of the problems to be resolved before world peace can be assured. Thus I do not think Lorenz is justified in inferring a 'blockage' of rational thought by innate mechanisms.

What, in conclusion, of the Ninth Reason? I have examined writings of Dawkins, Wilson and Lorenz because they are reputable scientists as well as being widely regarded as 'genetic determinists'. (Obviously the genetic determinist views of popularizers who lack scientific credentials are worthless in evaluating the Ninth Reason.) None of these writers denies that we have the reason and freedom to transcend genetic influences. Precisely because we can understand these influences we can transcend them.

It is odd that Dawkins, who is no dualist, should distinguish 'us' on one hand from 'our genes' on the other. Unless we want to endorse dualism, we must not think of our reason as something distinct from our inherited nature. The use we make of our reason is not inherited, but our powers of reason are. So the final, short answer to the Ninth Reason might be: our genes do not *exclude* free will; it is not even the case that we have free will *in spite of* our genes; rather, it is *because*, though obviously not only because, we have the genes we do that we have free will.

tenth reason: the past

All our choices and actions are the result of past events. We cannot alter the past. Hence we have no free will.

It is easy to feel passive in regard to the past. The past made us what we are now; we, on the other hand, can do nothing about the past. We are thus in an inferior position: the past controls us, we do not control it. However, it would be a mistake to suppose that because the past is outside our control, therefore the effects of the past on the future are also outside our control (see my discussion in chapter 3). The Tenth Reason is perhaps the First Reason over again: the past determines the future and if determinism is true, we cannot do anything but what we do do.

Marx, in a famous remark, said that 'the past sits like an Alp on the brains of the living'. Obviously we have to start with what we've got: the past determines our starting point and the means we have of dealing with it. But Marx certainly did not think that we do not have the freedom to change practices derived from the past. On the contrary.

We do not have free will in regard to past events. They are fixed. And this can certainly be cause for regret: 'If only I had done that!' But the past does not take away our freedom of will. Our will is directed towards the future not the past. R.E. Hobart puts the past in its place in these remarks:

> A man is a being with free will and responsibility; where this being came from, I repeat, is another story. The past finished its functions in the business when it generated him as he is. So far from interfering with him and coercing him, the past does not even exist. If we could imagine it as lingering on into the present, standing over against him and stretching out a ghostly hand to stay his arm, then indeed the past would be interfering with his liberty and responsibility. But so long as it and he are never on the scene together they cannot wrestle; the past cannot overpower him. The whole alarm is an evil dream, a nightmare due to the indigestion of words. The past has created, and left extant, a free-willed being.

There is nothing about the past as such which takes away our free will. If determinism can co-exist with free will, we need not worry about the past.

eleventh reason: luck
Everything that happens to us is a matter of luck. But luck is outside our control. Hence we have no free will.

The Eleventh Reason has been forcefully argued by John Hospers (in 1957). He invites us to consider someone who has been brought up in circumstances which have turned him into a spendthrift:

> But, one will say, he could have overcome his spendthrift tendencies; some people do. Quite true: some people do. they are lucky. They have it in them to overcome early deficiencies by exerting great effort, and they are capable of exerting the effort. Some of us, luckier still, can overcome them with but little effort; and a few, the luckiest, haven't the deficiencies to overcome. It's all a matter of luck. The least lucky are those who can't overcome them, even with great effort, and those who haven't the ability to exert the effort.
> But, one persists, it isn't a matter simply of luck; it *is* a matter of effort. Very well then, it's a matter of effort; without exerting that effort you may not overcome the deficiency. But whether

or not you are the kind of person who has it in him to exert the effort is a matter of luck.

This argument is seductive.   Luck becomes all-enveloping. Normally luck is contrasted with effort or skill, but Hospers argues that effort and skill are a matter of luck too. It is of no avail for a person to claim that she acquired a skill through hard work and dedication because it was a matter of luck that she had it in her to work hard and be dedicated. Since what we get as a result of good or bad luck is no credit or discredit to us, the omni-presence of luck excludes free will.

There seems, though, to be a flaw in Hospers' argument. He runs together the capacity or ability to make an effort on the one hand and actually making an effort on the other. But even if the former is a matter of luck, it does not follow that the latter is too. Consider this case: whether I am born blind is, from my point of view, just a matter of luck; it is not up to me, and I can neither be blamed nor praised. So the possession of this capacity, sight, is solely a matter of luck. But it does not follow that whether I exercise this capacity is also a matter of luck. On the contrary, it *is* up to me whether I use my eyes or not.

Consider another case: I am the world's best chess-player. Here again I have a certain capacity or ability, the ability to play chess better than anyone else. Is this a matter of luck? No, I worked hard. But my capacity to work hard, is that a matter of luck? No, I developed my capacity to work hard through will-power. But my capacity to use my will-power, is that a matter of luck? No, my parents taught me to be strong-willed. That was luck! If we push the questions back far enough we always get back to luck. After all, it's a matter of luck that each of us exists at all. But, again, the fact that my capacity to work hard ultimately rests on my luck in being born does not imply that it was just a matter of luck that I actually did work hard. Hospers seems to believe that if my actions ultimately depend on luck, then they are infected with luck, as it were, all the way down.

There is an explanation of why Hospers should run together the capacity to do something and actually doing it, namely an allegiance to the First Reason. Suppose we accept the view (discussed in chapter 4) that I cannot act otherwise than I do. Then, if I did not work hard, I could not have worked hard. From this it follows (by logic) that if I could have worked hard, then I did work hard; and therefore, if it is a matter of luck that I could have worked hard, it is a matter of luck that I did work hard.

But unless we adopt the First Reason, we are not entitled to say of someone that just because he did not work hard (as a result of upbringing or whatever), therefore he *could not* have worked hard. On the other hand, if we have a good reason for saying that someone really is *incapable* of working hard or lying, and if that incapacity is in no way due to him then we would have to say that this incapacity is a matter of luck, in which case he cannot be blamed for it (or, in George Washington's case, praised).

To conclude: luck certainly plays a part in our lives, but unless it leaves us literally incapable of choosing to do something we might choose to do, it does not take away our free will.

twelfth reason: the unconscious

Our unconscious determines what we do; but the unconscious is not under our control. Hence we do not have free will.

This Reason, like the Eleventh, has been forcefully presented by John Hospers (in 1950). Hospers says that 'what people want when they talk about freedom and what they hold to when they champion it, is the idea that the *conscious* will is the master of their destiny': but this they cannot have:

> To be sure, the domination by the unconscious in the case of 'normal' individuals is somewhat more benevolent than the tyranny and despotism exercised in neurotic cases, and therefore the former have evoked less comment; but the principle remains in all cases the same: the unconscious is the master of every fate and the captain of every soul.

Hospers suggests that 'a person is free only to the extent that his acts are *not unconsciously determined at all*, be the unconscious benevolent *or* malevolent':

If this is the criterion, psychoanalysts would say, most human behaviour cannot be called free at all: our impulses and volitions having to do with our basic attitudes towards life, whether we are optimists or pessimists, tough-minded or tender-minded, whether our tempers are quick or slow, whether we are 'naturally self-seeking' or 'naturally benevolent' (and *all the acts consequent upon these things*), what things annoy us, whether we take to blondes or brunettes [or baldies], old or young, whether we become philosophers or artists or businessmen – all this has its basis in the unconscious.

But should we adopt this criterion of freedom? It seems to be the First Reason over again with determination by the unconscious replacing determinism in general. Earlier in his article Hospers states his claim differently: that if an adult's behaviour is the *inevitable* consequence of early childhood experiences, over which she or he has no control, then that behaviour is not freely willed. This is certainly acceptable. But we cannot infer inevitability from determinism (see the Third Reason).

If Hospers could show that behaviour we normally take to be free is in fact *wholly* determined by the unconscious, then the Twelfth Reason would have some plausibility. But this goes beyond what psychoanalysts usually say. The principal claim of psychoanalysis is not that we are unfree, but that we can become free by understanding and coming to terms with our unconscious. Even if our acts are determined by our unconscious, so long as our unconscious is working in parallel, as it were, with our conscious, we are free.

thirteenth reason: compulsion

All our choices and actions are compelled by internal or external forces. Compulsion excludes free will. Hence we have no free will.

Philosophers generally agree that compulsion excludes (or at least reduces) free will. For example, Moritz Schlick wrote (in the 1930s):

Freedom means the opposite of compulsion; a man is *free* if he does not act under *compulsion*, and he is compelled or unfree when he is hindered from without in the realization of his natural desires. Hence he is unfree when he is locked up, or chained,

> or when someone forces him at the point of a gun to do what otherwise he would not do.

This recalls Hume's definition of liberty (see chapter 2). Schlick extends 'external' hindrances to include alcohol and drugs (if taken involuntarily) and mental illness. A.J. Ayer (in 1946) explicitly allows for psychological, as well as external, forms of compulsion:

> A kleptomaniac is not a free agent, in respect of his stealing, because he does not go through any process of deciding whether or not to steal. Or rather, if he does go through such a process, it is irrelevant to his behaviour. Whatever he resolved to do, he would steal all the same. And it is this that distinguishes him from the ordinary thief.

But why stop here? John Hospers comments:

> Many voluntary acts came to be recognized, at least in some circles, as compelled by the unconscious. Some philosophers recognized this too...The usual examples, such as the kleptomaniac and the schizophrenic, apparently satisfy most philosophers, and with these exceptions removed, the rest of mankind is permitted to wander in the vast and alluring fields of freedom and responsibility. So far, the inroads upon freedom left the vast majority of humanity untouched; they began to hit home when psychiatrists began to realize, though philosophers did not, that the domination of the conscious by the unconscious extended, not merely to a few exceptional individuals, but to all human beings.

If we cannot distinguish between causes which compel and causes which do not, and if we also accept that all our choices and actions are caused and that compulsion excludes free will, then we shall have to accept the Thirteenth Reason. The Thirteenth Reason provides an argument in favour of the First Reason – which explains why philosophers who accept both determinism *and* free will (Schlick, Ayer and Hobart, for example) are keen to establish that there is a distinction between compelling causes and causes which do not compel.

Hobart rejects the Thirteenth Reason on the ground that it leads to the absurd conclusion that we are compelled by our wishes and preferences:

In fact, the moral self is the wishing self. The wishes are its own. It cannot be described as under their dominion, for it has no separate predilections to be overborne by them; they themselves are its predilections. To fancy that because the person acts according to them he is compelled, a slave, the victim of a power from whose clutches he cannot extricate himself, is a confusion of ideas, a mere slip of the mind. The answer that has ordinarily been given is surely correct; all compulsion is causation, but not all causation is compulsion. Seize a man and violently force him to do something, and he is compelled – also caused – to do it. But induce him to do it by giving him reasons and his doing it is caused but not compelled.

Therefore the Thirteenth Reason must be rejected.

However, we must, I think, concede in favour of the Thirteenth Reason that it is very difficult to draw a hard and fast line between causes which compel and causes which do not. After discovering that chemical pollution which causes miscarriages is ineradicable, a paint company offers to keep female workers in their jobs if they agree to be sterilized. An offer? Or a compulsive threat? (Compare the classic line from *The Godfather:* 'I made him an offer he couldn't refuse'.) However, it does not follow from the fact that because it is hard to draw a clear line between compulsion and absence of compulsion that there is no line to be drawn. It is hard to draw a clear line between night and day; but it does not follow that there is no difference between them.

We must also concede in favour of the Thirteenth Reason that freedom is sometimes an illusion: we may be subject to constraint or compulsion without realizing it, as, perhaps, in the case of post-hypnotic suggestion. But again it does not follow that there is no difference between compulsion and its absence.

We may also (but perhaps less definitely) concede the existence of 'psychological compulsions'. But if we follow Ayer in saying that such compulsions always express themselves in behaviour *whatever* one may resolve, then it is clearly wrong to say that all our motivations compel us. If it is said that we are powerless to act against our motivations because we cannot act otherwise than we do, then this is no longer the Thirteenth Reason but (again) the First (see chapter 4).

fourteenth reason: manipulation

We are all manipulated from the moment we are born to the moment we die. Hence we have no free will.

e are born to the moment we die. Hence we have no free will.

The paradigm of manipulation is Huxley's Brave New World where everyone is indoctrinated from birth. It is for their own good of course; but surely they are not free. Manipulation is insidious because we do not know it is going on. Many studies have been made, for instance, of the ways in which advertisers manipulate us into buying their products. So whatever its motivation, manipulation is offensive. If it is done for our own good it is patronizing; if for others' good it is exploitation.

Manipulation was the method of education favoured by Rousseau in preference to Locke's idea of appealing to childrens' reason ('I see nothing more stupid than children who have been reasoned with,' Rousseau said):

> Let him [the child] believe that he is always in control, though it is always you who really are. There is no subjugation so perfect as that which keeps the appearance of freedom, for in that way one makes the will itself captive. The poor child, knowing nothing, able to do nothing, having learned nothing, is he not at your mercy? Can you not arrange everything in the world around him? Can you not influence him as you wish? His work, his play, his pleasures, his pains, are not all these in your hands and without his knowing? Doubtless he ought to do only what he wants; but he ought to want to do only what you want him to do. He ought not to take a step which you have not foreseen; he ought not to open his mouth without your knowing what he will say.

In fact, it is hard to imagine an institutionalized form of education which does not depend on manipulation. If we find this acceptable, it is because we can think of no better system and because such manipulation is confined to children.

Manipulation is opposed to rationality in two ways. First, it depends on non-rational means to get us to do things. Second, it relies on our not using our reason to see that we are being manipulated. But manipulation is vulnerable to counter-attack precisely because of these two features. First, as rational creatures we have an aversion to being made to do things by non-rational factors. Second, as rational creatures we retain the wherewithal to detect manipulation. ('You can't fool all of the people all of the time.') So long as we retain this aversion and this wherewithal, manipulation will not destroy, though it may reduce, our free will.

fifteenth reason: irresistible desires
We cannot resist acting on our desires. Hence we have no free will.

If determinism is true and if it implies that we cannot act contrary to the desires we act on, then all desires are irresistible. This is the First Reason again. But it does not seem that all our desires are irresistible. Some desires can be resisted by considering the unfortunate consequences of satisfying them. If one could not overcome a desire however much one tried to persuade oneself that the desire was a bad one and however many reasons there were against it, then perhaps such a desire is indeed irresistible. But that is not true of our desires generally. An irresistible desire is a desire (it need not be *impulsive*, we might harbour it for days or even years) which is not under our rational control. Unless we follow the First Reason and say that because of determinism we cannot control our desires, only a few (and perhaps no) desires will be irresistible.

sixteenth reason: strongest desire
We always act according to our strongest desire; we have no choice. Hence we have no free will.

Even if we can resist some desires, can we resist our strongest desires? If we have free will shouldn't we be able to act against our inclinations however strong they are? But some have argued that we cannot act against our strongest desires, from which it may be inferred that we do not have free will.

Interestingly, some defenders of free will have held that we cannot act against our strongest desires. For instance, John Stuart Mill wrote:

> I therefore dispute altogether that we are conscious of being able to act in opposition to the strongest present desire or aversion. The difference between a bad and a good man is not

that the latter acts in opposition to his strongest desires; it is that his desire to do right, and his aversion to doing wrong, are strong enough to overcome, and in the case of perfect virtue, to silence, any other desire or aversion which may conflict with them.

But perhaps one could be good without being free.

W.D. Ross (in the 1930's) also argued, like Mill, that we always act according to our strongest desire. He rejects 'the belief that, the circumstances being what they are, and I being what I am, with that whole system of beliefs, desires and dispositions which compose my nature, it is objectively possible for me here and now to do either of two or more acts':

> This is *not* possible, because whatever act I do, it must be because there is in me, as I am now, a stronger impulse to do that act than to do any other. Everyone would probably agree that this is so when neither of the two acts is being thought of as a duty. It would be agreed that then we must do the act, to which we have the strongest desire, or rather the act to which the strongest mass of desires leads us. But it is equally true when one of the two acts *is* thought of as a duty, even if we take the view that what impels us to do an act of duty as such is not a desire but a specific emotion of respect or reverence. For even so we shall do the duty if and only if this emotion constitutes an impulse to do the act of duty, stronger than the impulse which moves us toward doing any other act. And if act *A* can only be done if I have a stronger impulse to do act *A* than to do act *B*, and if act *B* can only be done if I have a stronger impulse to do act *B* than to do act *A*, it cannot be the case I can here and now equally do either act. It must follow from my nature and my present condition that I must do act *A*, or else that I must do act *B*.

Ross nevertheless believes in free will since he considers the freedom to act against one's strongest desire a 'variety of free will not worth wanting' (to use D.C. Dennett's phrase). Ross poses the question, 'Would there be any moral value in a freedom to do, in such a case, what we do not most wish to do?' and responds, 'It would be a freedom to act for no reason, and indeed against reason.'

However, Ross is confused. In fact, while defending free will on the one hand, he agrees with supporters of the First

Reason that, if determinism is true, we cannot act otherwise than we do. He accepts the view that 'act *A* can only be done if I have a stronger impulse to do act *A* than act *B*'. But what a defender of both determinism and free will should say is that act *A* *will* be done only if I have a stronger impulse to do it, but it *can* be done even if I have a stronger impulse to do something else. All that is required is that I *can* change my preferences and thereby come to have a stronger impulse to do act *A*. (For further discussion, see chapter 4.)

R.E. Hobart, also a determinist, presents the opposite opinion to Ross:

> I can will anything, and can will effectively anything that my body will enact. I can will it despite an inclination to the contrary of any strength you please – strength as felt by me before decision. We all know cases where we have resisted impulses of great strength in this sense and we can imagine them still stronger. I have the power to do it, and shall do it, shall exercise that power, if I prefer.

Hobart suggests that people have misunderstood the words 'strongest desire'.

If 'strongest desire' means 'the desire one acts on', then of course one never acts in opposition to one's strongest desire, because that would involve acting contrary to the desire on which one acts; and this is self-contradictory.

If 'strongest desire' means 'the desire one would act on unless some new desire intervened', then one certainly can act against one's strongest desire, by forming some new, perhaps more rational, desire.

If 'strongest desire' means 'most intense desire', then again one can act against one's strongest desire because sometimes the most intense desires are not the most prudent and one may choose (unwisely perhaps!) to follow one's most prudent desire.

If 'strongest desire' is understood in the first sense, then it is no limitation on our freedom that we cannot act against our strongest desire (just as it is no limitation on our freedom that we cannot make a round square). If 'strongest desire' is interpreted in either of the other ways, then we can act against our strongest desire. The only argument for saying that we cannot is the argument for the First Reason that we cannot act otherwise than we do (see chapter 4).

seventeenth reason: selfishness

All our actions are selfish. We cannot act from any other motive. Therefore we have no free will.

The view that all our motivation is selfish is known as psychological egoism among philosophers. To some it seems self-evident: how could we be motivated towards something that does not benefit ourselves?

To others it seems equally absurd: do we not often want to do things for the benefit of others rather than ourselves? To which the reply comes back: but why do we want to do things for others? Only because it gives us pleasure, or satisfaction; so it's all a matter of our own self-interest. This point is illustrated in a story about Abraham Lincoln:

> Mr. Lincoln once remarked to a fellow-passenger on an old-time mud-coach that all men were prompted by selfishness in doing good. His fellow-passenger was antagonizing this position when they were passing over a corduroy bridge that spanned a slough. As they crossed this bridge they espied an old razor-backed sow on the bank making a terrible noise because her pigs had got into the slough and were in danger of drowning. As the old coach began to climb the hill, Mr. Lincoln called out, 'Driver, can't you stop just a moment?' Then Mr. Lincoln jumped out, ran back and lifted the little pigs out of the mud and water and placed them on the bank. When he returned, his companion remarked: 'Now Abe, where does selfishness come in on this little episode?' 'Why, bless your soul Ed, that was the very essence of selfishness. I should have had no peace of mind all day had I gone on and left that suffering old sow worrying over those pigs. I did it to get peace of mind, don't you see?'

Ed should have replied: 'You would have felt distress all day, if you hadn't helped the pigs, *because* you were motivated to help them. You were *not* motivated to help them *because* you would have felt distress all day if you hadn't; you were motivated by your good nature.' Aristotle remarks that the good man takes pleasure in doing good things; consequently he feels distress if he doesn't. It does not follow that he does good things *in order to* avoid feeling distress.

The psychological egoist can rightly point out that whenever we want something we must see some good in it; it must seem good or worthwhile in some way from our point of view. However, 'good from our point of view' does not necessarily mean 'good *for us'*. Helping suffering pigs seemed worthwhile from Lincoln's point of view; perhaps he considered unnecessary suffering an intrinsic evil to be avoided if possible. But it does not follow that he thought there was some benefit *to him* in helping the pigs. Someone else might be quite indifferent to suffering pigs; from that person's point of view their suffering is not important enough to be worth doing anything about. The difference between Lincoln and that person is not that one thought helping the pigs would benefit himself and the other didn't, but that they had different points of view on what was worth doing.

The psychological egoist can rightly point out that there are some people who do good deeds for clearly selfish reasons; they don't care about others' welfare; they just want gratitude, fame, respect, a knighthood, etc. But it is fallacious to argue that therefore *everyone* is selfish. It is only because we distinguish between those who do not care about others and those who do that we call the former selfish. This implies that the latter are not selfish. The proponent of the Seventeenth Reason is attempting to extend the orbit of selfishness to include all actions, just as the proponent of the Thirteenth Reason attempted to extend the orbit of compulsion to include all actions. But we need some further reason for accepting these extensions besides the fact that *some* actions are selfish, or compelled.

Even if we are thoroughly convinced by the psychological egoist's argument, I think it has no consequences for free will whatsoever. For if our 'egoism' is as much catered to by our being altruistic (in the ordinary sense) as being selfish (in the ordinary sense), then our ability to choose and our range of options are not one whit diminished by the fact that we are 'selfish' in the egoist's sense. Our free will is limited only if there are things we cannot do or choose. But on the egoist's view, all choices are equally egoistic; hence there is nothing we cannot do or choose.

eighteenth reason: ignorance

We never act in full knowledge of the circumstances and consequences of our actions. Hence we do not act freely.

'And ye shall know the truth, and the truth shall make you free' (St. John's Gospel, chapter 8, verse 32). Socrates and Aristotle thought that ignorance makes our acts involuntary. And certainly we do not hold people responsible for unforeseeable accidents where they could not have known what would happen.

The Eighteenth Reason seems especially plausible in regard to the past. Knowing what we now know, we would often have chosen differently. Hence our past choice appears to be not a free choice but the product of ignorance. What we forget is that it was nevertheless our choice. The fact that we would not make the same choice now does not imply that it was not ourselves who made the choice then. And if it was our choice, then it might have been a free choice, despite our ignorance. Of course if our ignorance were the result of manipulation, our choice might not have been free (see Fourteenth Reason). But it would be strange to claim that we *never* know what we're doing.

review of the eighteen reasons

We have now examined eighteen reasons for not believing that we have free will. There could be other reasons perhaps; but I think they could probably be fitted in under one or other of our Reasons. Should we now not believe that we have free will?

Certainly we do not have free will in regard to everything. For instance, we cannot change the past. Some things are going to happen inevitably, and we have no control over them. Sometimes we are subject to compulsion which takes away our freedom. And so on.

But we have found only one all-embracing reason which seriously threatens to disprove the claim that we have free will. And that is the First Reason: thus it turns out that the First

Reason is not only the most important historically but the most important as far as answering our question is concerned.

Philosophers sometimes lament the fact that their discussions are inconclusive. If 'inconclusive' means that we cannot settle the issue to *everyone's* satisfaction, then, yes, philosophical discussions, including ours, are inconclusive. Equally rational and intelligent people can and do disagree about what the right answer is. But philosophical discussions are not inconclusive in the sense that they do not reach any conclusions. It is just that everyone, after reviewing the arguments and thinking about them, has to reach his or her own conclusion.

notes

Second Reason
St. Augustine. The quotations here and elsewhere in this chapter are from 'The Freedom of the Will' in his *The City of God.*

Necessity. There are many fallacies involving 'necessity'; it is a very tricky notion from a logical point of view. (i) The statement, 'It is necessarily true that either this is the case or that is the case,' does not imply the statement, 'Either this is necessarily the case or that is necessarily the case.' (ii) The distinction between a 'necessary truth' and a 'necessary consequence' is important. A necessary truth is one which must be true. A necessary consequence is a statement that follows necessarily from other statements, i.e. it is a necessary truth that *if* they are true, it is true. A necessary consequence need not itself be true, let alone necessarily true.

Sir Arthur Eddington, 1882-1944, British physicist, astronomer, and scientific popularizer, author of *The Nature of the Physical World* (1928).

R.E. Hobart, alias Dickinson S. Miller, American philosopher, 1868-1963. The quotation from Eddington, Hobart's discussion of it, and other quotations from Hobart elsewhere in this chapter, are from his article 'Free Will as Involving Determination and Inconceivable Without It'.

For further discussion of fatalism see G. Ryle 'It Was to Be', and A. J. Ayer 'Fatalism'.

Third Reason
D.C. Dennett, contemporary American philosopher. The quotations are from *Elbow Room*, p. 124 and 127 note.

Historical inevitability. For an extended attack on this idea, which also includes an attack on determinism, see Isaiah Berlin, *Historical Inevitability.*

Skinner's Walden Two: see ch. 1.

Fourth Reason
Pierre de Laplace, French mathematician. The quotation is from his *Analytic Theory of Probability* (1820).

Fifth Reason
Descartes (see ch. 2). The quotations are from his *Discourse on Method,* Part V.

Minds and machines. See Geoffrey Brown's book in this series, *Minds, Brains and Machines*. For an argument that we could not be mechanisms, see Malcolm, 'The Conceivability of Mechanism'. For a reply see Goldman, 'The Compatibility of Mechanism and Purpose'. See also Dennett, *Elbow Room.*

Sixth Reason
Alan Turing, 20th century British mathematician and computer scientist. For his discussion of Lady Lovelace's objection, see 'Computing Machinery and Intelligence'.

Seventh Reason
John Stuart Mill, 1806-73, prominent English philosopher, author of many works, including *An Examination of Sir William Hamilton's Philosophy;* the quotations here and elsewhere in this chapter are from 'The Freedom of Will' in Vol. II.

Aristotle (see ch. 2). This quotation is from his *Nicomachean Ethics,* Bk. III, ch. 5.

Paul Edwards, 20th century American philosopher. The quotation is from his 'Hard and Soft Determinism'.

A.J. Ayer, prominent 20th century English philosopher. The quotations here and elsewhere in this chapter are from his 'Freedom and Necessity'.

Eighth Reason
B. F. Skinner (see ch. 1). The quotations are from his *Science and Human Behaviour,* ch. 3, and *Beyond Freedom and Dignity,* ch. 3.

D.C. Dennett. The quotations are from *Elbow Room,* p. 59.

Ninth Reason
Richard Dawkins, contemporary English scientist, author of *The Selfish Gene* and other works on evolutionary biology. The quotations are from *The Selfish Gene,* pp. ix, 2, 3, 215.

E.O. Wilson, contemporary American scientist, author of *Sociobiology: The New Synthesis, On Human Nature*, and other works.

Konrad Lorenz, 20th century Austrian scientist, author of the delightful *King Solomon's Ring* and the controversial *On Aggression* (1963). The quotations are from his article 'Part and Parcel in Animal and Human Societies'.

For further discussion of genetic determinism, see Mary Midgley, *Beast and Man* and 'Gene-Juggling', and Roger Trigg, *The Shaping of Man.*

Tenth Reason
Karl Marx, 1818-83, founder of Marxism.

Eleventh Reason
John Hospers, 20th century American philosopher. The quotation is from 'What Means This Freedom?'

Twelfth Reason
John Hospers. The quotations here and in the Thirteenth Reason are from 'Free Will and Psychoanalysis'.

Thirteenth Reason
Moritz Schlick, 20th century Austrian philosopher. The quotation is from 'When Is a Man Responsible?'

Fourteenth Reason
Aldous Huxley, see ch. 1.

Jean-Jacques Rousseau, 1712-78, philosopher and political theorist, born in Geneva, author of *Emile: or On Education;* the quotations are from Book II.

John Locke (see ch. 2). His principal work on education was *Some Thoughts Concerning Education* (1690).

For further discussion of manipulation, see J. Glover, *Responsibility* and P.S. Greenspan, 'Behaviour Control and Freedom of Action'.

Fifteenth Reason
Irresistible desires. See Kenny, *Freewill and Responsibility* for discussion.

Sixteenth Reason
W. D. Ross, 20th century British moral philosopher. The quotations are from his *Foundations of Ethics*, pp. 222-51.

D.C. Dennett. 'The Varieties of Free Will Worth Wanting' is the subtitle of his *Elbow Room*.

Seventeenth Reason
Lincoln. This perhaps apocryphal story originally appeared in the *Springfield Monitor*. It is quoted from Joel Feinberg's essay 'Psychological Egoism', which contains a full discussion of the topic.

Eighteenth Reason
Socrates and Aristotle, see ch. 2.

6: four reasons for believing in free will

We must now consider some reasons for believing that we do have free will.

first reason: consciousness of free will
We are conscious of being free. We feel free. Hence we have free will.

We feel free when we are doing what we want to do. Thus it is not surprising that some philosophers, for example Hobbes, have identified freedom with doing what one wants. But this is a mistake. If someone has been brainwashed into wanting something, then she may feel free but she will not be free. Free will is not just doing what one wants, but being free to have one's own wants, not dictated by others. In Skinner's *Walden Two* people feel free because all control there is 'non-aversive', i.e. it does not use measures which arouse resistance or are unpleasant. Manipulation is a far less obvious threat to freedom than force or threats because we may feel free when we're being manipulated though not when being forced or threatened. But feeling free does not prove that we are free. Even a happy slave can feel free, but he's still a slave.

Philosophers have sometimes suggested that we know from our consciousness of willing and acting that we have free will. Henry Sidgwick wrote in the 19th century:

> We must conclude, then, that against the formidable array of cumulative evidence offered for Determinism [i.e. the First Reason against free will] there is but one opposing argument of

real force: the immediate affirmation of consciousness in the moment of deliberate action. And certainly, in the case of actions in which I have a distinct consciousness of choosing between alternatives of conduct, one of which I conceive as right and reasonable, I find it impossible not to think that I can now choose to do what I so conceive, however strong may be my inclination to act unreasonably, and however uniformly I may have yielded to such inclinations in the past...I recognize that each concession to vicious desire makes the difficulty of resisting it greater when the desire recurs; but the difficulty always seems to remain separated by an impassable gulf from impossibility.

J.S. Mill disputed, however, whether there is such an 'immediate affirmation of consciousness':

To be conscious of free will, must mean, to be conscious, before I have decided, that I am able to decide either way. Exception may be taken *in limine* [at the outset] to the use of the word 'consciousness' in such an application. Consciousness tells me what I do or feel. But what I am *able* to do, is not a subject of consciousness. Consciousness is not prophetic; we are conscious of what is, not of what will or can be.

In Mill's view our experience suggests that we can act otherwise only in the sense that we would act otherwise if conditions (physical and/or psychological) were different:

When we think of ourselves hypothetically as having acted otherwise than we did, we always suppose a difference in the antecedents: we picture ourselves as having known something that we did not know, or not known something that we did know; which is a difference in the external motives; or as having desired something, or disliked something, more or less than we did; which is a difference in the internal motives.

Mill here expresses the view that our consciousness of being free is quite compatible with a deterministic account of human action.

C.A. Campbell, however, thinks that introspection, i.e. careful attention to our conscious experience, indicates that our will is not determined by antecedent factors:

In the situation of moral conflict, then, I (as agent) have before my mind a course of action *X*, which I believe to be my duty; and also a course of action *Y*, incompatible with *X*, which I feel to be that which I most strongly desire. *Y* is, as it is sometimes expressed, 'in the line of least resistance' for me – the course which I am aware I should take if I let my purely desiring nature operate without hindrance. It is the course towards which I am aware that my *character,* as so far formed, naturally inclines me. Now, as actually engaged in this situation, I find that I cannot help believing that I *can* rise to duty and choose *X*; the 'rising to duty' being effected by what is commonly called 'effort of will'. And I further find, if I ask myself just what it is I am believing when I believe that I 'can' rise to duty, that I cannot help believing that it lies with me here and now, quite absolutely, which of two genuinely open possibilities I adopt; whether, that is, I make the effort of will and choose *X*, or, on the other hand, let my desiring nature, my character as so far formed, 'have its way', and choose *Y*, the course 'in the line of least resistance'...

   Now here is the vital point. No matter which course, *X* or *Y*, I choose in this situation, I cannot doubt, *qua* [as a] practical being engaged in it, that my choice is *not* just the expression of my formed character, and yet is a choice made by my *self*. For suppose I make the effort and choose *X* (my 'duty'). Since my very purpose in making the 'effort' is to enable me to act against the existing 'set' of desire, which is the expression of my character as so far formed, I cannot possibly regard the act itself as the expression of my *character*. On the other hand, introspection makes it equally clear that I am certain that it is *I* who choose; that the act is not an 'accident', but is genuinely *my* act. Or suppose that I choose *Y* (the end of 'strongest desire'). The course chosen here is, it is true, in conformity with my 'character'. But since I find myself unable to doubt that I *could* have made the effort and chosen *X*, I cannot possibly regard the choice of *Y* as *just* the expression of my character. Yet here again I find that I cannot doubt that the choice is *my* choice, a choice for which *I* am justly to be blamed.

Campbell's conscious experience thus indicates to him that by an effort of will he can create 'a definite rupture in the causal continuity of past and present': 'The effort is felt, then, as self-determined, and yet as not determined by the self's character as so far formed, not, i.e., causally continuous with the self's past.' Campbell calls this 'contra-causal freedom'. He allows the possibility that his experience may be illusory, but says that 'the only direct evidence there *could* be for a creative activity like "free will" is an intuition of the practical consciousness'.

The problem with Campbell's view is that it is difficult to see how we can be aware of the *absence* of causes. How could we *feel* that we have 'contra-causal freedom'? Schlick for instance writes: 'This feeling is not the consciousness of the absence of a cause, but of something altogether different, namely, of *freedom*, which consists in the fact that I can act as I desire.' Certainly one can fail to be aware that there are causes operating, but that does not imply that there are no causes operating.

Campbell seems to have a rather Kantian view of the situation. On the one side there is the agent's character (Kant's 'empirical' self) which is the product of past causal factors and on the other side there is the agent's self (Kant's 'rational' self) which is exempt, or can exempt itself, from causation. Now, we can agree with Campbell that one's character is not the same as one's self (see the discussion of the Seventh Reason against free will). But it does not follow that one's self and efforts of will are not causally determined. Why could it not be that when I 'rise to duty' my so rising is causally determined, though I may not be aware that it is?

When is a person aware of causal factors influencing him? I suggest it is only when those factors appear *external* in some way to the person. If I wholeheartedly want to do something, then I don't think of myself as being caused to do it. But if I am aware of factors in my make-up which I do not approve of but which influence my actions, then I may experience a causal influence as though from outside myself ('The devil made me do it'). If I lose my temper when I know I shouldn't, I may think of myself as being caused to lose my temper.

Thus, when Campbell thinks of 'my desiring nature, my character as so far formed', as inclining me in one direction while *I* can rise to duty and do the opposite, he is thinking of his 'desiring nature' as something external to himself and hence he experiences it as a causal influence. But since he identifies himself with the self that can rise to duty, he does not experience himself as being *caused* to rise to duty. In the case of a reformed Puritan it might be just the opposite: 'I felt my dutiful nature inclining me to say No, while at the same time I knew I could by an effort of will let myself go and have a good time.' In neither case would we be justified in inferring that the effort of will, just because it was opposed to one's desiring or dutiful nature (as the case may be), was not the product of past causes. But because it is *my* effort of will, I would not experience it as caused.

The upshot of this discussion is that our experiences of being 'caused' to do things are not a good guide to what is actually happening. We must bear in mind Spinoza's assertion that 'men believe themselves to be free simply because they are conscious of their actions, knowing nothing of the causes by which they are determined'.

On the other hand, if we have no good reason to believe it is illusory, our consciousness of being free may be a good reason for believing that we are. Dr. Johnson remarked, 'Sir, we know our will is free, and there's an end on't.' He also remarked, 'All theory is against the freedom of the will; all experience for it.'

second reason: choice and decision

Choice always involves alternatives. We make choices for ourselves and reach decisions by ourselves. Hence we have free will.

Choice and decision are everywhere in our lives because at the very least we are always choosing between acting and not acting, deciding to do or not to do. Choice and decision by their very nature seem to imply that I *can* choose or decide to do something other than what I do choose or decide to do. Can we then conclude from the fact that we make choices and decisions, that we have free will?

However, surely lots of animals make choices without having free will. My cat may choose to stay out all night or not, depending on her whim. Any animal endowed with an appropriate flexibility of behaviour can choose to do a thing or not. Do they have free will then? If we want to say they do not (and perhaps we do not), it is probably because they do not, we suppose, go through any real decision-making process. This suggests that we shall have to be more specific about what constitutes a *free* choice or decision.

Choice always involves alternatives.

First, though, I want to ask whether choice does imply that we can choose otherwise than we do. We saw, in chapter 4, that, according to some, if determinism is true we *cannot* choose otherwise than we do. Even if we are not convinced by this argument, it may still seem that choice does not imply that we actually can choose otherwise than we do, but only that we *think* we can.

For instance it might be said that someone who has been subjected to post-hypnotic suggestion might think she is freely choosing to do something and that she could choose to do something else instead, when in fact this is not the case. But is such a person really choosing? She might *think* she is choosing and therefore think that she could choose otherwise; but if the 'choice' is a direct result of the hypnotism, it would not appear to be a real choice.

There is a further argument, proposed by Harry Frankfurt (in 1969), which suggests that one can choose without being able to choose otherwise. He imagines the following sort of case:

Suppose someone – Black, let us say – wants Jones to perform a certain action. Black is prepared to go to considerable lengths to get his way, but he prefers to avoid showing his hand unnecessarily. So he waits until Jones is about to make up his mind what to do, and he does nothing unless it is clear to him (Black is an excellent judge of such things) that Jones is going to decide to do something *other* than what he wants him to do. If it does become clear that Jones is going to decide to do something else, Black takes effective steps to ensure that Jones decides to do, and that he does do, what he wants him to do. Whatever Jones's initial preferences and inclinations, then, Black will have his way.

We may suppose that Black has a method of manipulating Jones' brain, or something else equally effective. Now, Jones may, without any interference from Black, choose to do what Black wants him to do. But he cannot choose to do anything else. So choosing does not imply being able to choose otherwise. At the same time, though, Jones does think he is able to choose otherwise and thus he is genuinely choosing.

Frankfurt's argument is appealing but perhaps inconclusive. My own feeling is that so long as Jones is genuinely choosing and Black is not interfering, then there are two courses of action open to Jones and he can choose either. At the same time it is true that Jones *will be* prevented from choosing the alternative Black doesn't like and in this sense he cannot (is unable to) choose that alternative. What this shows is that if a person is genuinely choosing then she can choose otherwise so far as her internal psychology is concerned – but an external force might prevent her from choosing otherwise in fact.

Consequently, the fact that I choose to do something does not prove that I am free. An example of John Locke's illustrates this. He wrote:

> Suppose a man be carried, whilst fast asleep, into a room, where is a person he longs to see and speak with, and be there locked fast in, beyond his power to get out; he awakes, and is glad to find himself in so desirable company, which he stays willingly in, i.e., prefers his stay to going away. I ask, is not this stay voluntary? I think nobody will doubt it; and yet, being locked fast in, it is evident he is not at liberty not to stay, he has not freedom to be gone.

At the same time it is plausible to say, if we exclude such external obstacles, that genuinely choosing implies being able to choose otherwise than one does.

In order to be 'genuinely choosing' the following conditions must be fulfilled: First, the person must have normal decision-making capacities, i.e. she must be capable of deciding what to do on the basis of reasons for and against different courses of action. Second, the person must be able to make use of those capacities. For instance, she must not be asleep, in a coma, in a state of uncontrollable panic, or subject to irresistible coercion. Third, the person must not be subject to external influences which impair her normal decision-making processes, such as post-hypnotic suggestion or scientists interfering with her brain.

If these conditions are fulfilled (and forgetting for the moment the argument from determinism), we may say that a person who does one thing could have chosen to do something else instead. It seems plausible to say that such a person has free will.

third reason: second-order desires

We not only have desires, we have second-order desires (i.e. desires *about* our desires). Hence we have free will.

The connection between second-order desires and free will has been argued by Harry Frankfurt (in 1971):

> Besides wanting and choosing and being moved *to do* this or that, men may also want to have (or not to have) certain desires and motives. They are capable of wanting to be different, in their preferences and purposes, from what they are. Many animals appear to have the capacity for what I shall call 'first-order desires' or 'desires of the first order', which are simply desires to do or not to do one thing or another. No animal other than man, however, appears to have the capacity for reflective self-evaluation that is manifested in the formation of second-order desires.

If I just want to do something, that is a first-order desire. But if I want not to want to do it, that is a second-order desire. For instance, I may want to eat more than is good for me; but I may also have the desire not to want to eat more than is good for me.

Frankfurt distinguishes two sorts of second-order desire. The first is when a person 'wants simply to have a certain desire'; the second is when a person 'wants a certain desire to be his will', that is to say, he wants it to be 'an *effective* desire – one that moves (or will or would move) a person all the way to action'. Frankfurt calls the latter 'second-order volitions'. Some creatures have desires but do not have second-order volitions. Frankfurt fittingly calls them 'wantons'.

Frankfurt claims that 'It is only because a person has volitions of the second order that he is capable both of enjoying and of lacking freedom of the will':

> It is in securing the conformity of his will to his second-order volitions, then, that a person exercises freedom of the will. And it is in the discrepancy between his will and his second-order volitions, or in his awareness that their coincidence is not his own doing but only a happy chance, that a person who does not have this freedom feels its lack.

Frankfurt illustrates this with an example of an unwilling drug addict:

> The unwilling addict has conflicting first-order desires: he wants to take the drug, and he also wants to refrain from taking it. In addition to these first-order desires, however, he has a volition of the second order. He is not a neutral with regard to the conflict between his desire to take the drug and his desire to refrain from taking it. It is the latter desire, and not the former, that he wants to constitute his will; it is the latter desire, rather than the former, that he wants to be effective and to provide the purpose that he will seek to realize in what he actually does...
>
> The unwilling addict's will is not free. This is shown by the fact that it is not the will he wants.

On the other hand, if the unwilling addict were to succeed in making his desire to give up drugs effective (thus conforming his will to his second-order volition), then he would be exercising freedom of will.

Undoubtedly Frankfurt has identified an important aspect of free will. Free will is not simply doing what one wants; it

involves control over one's wants, the ability to make either of
two conflicting desires one's will, i.e. the desire on which one
acts. Thus if a person would always act on a particular want
(*W*), even if he had a second-order volition not to act on want
W, then he would lack free will.

However, Frankfurt's account does not seem to provide a
sufficient condition of having free will: a person could have
second-order volitions, and could act according to these second-
order volitions, but nevertheless not have free will. For instance, his second-order volitions might have been implanted
in him by hypnosis or brain-washing; he might not be free to
have a different second-order volition, and thus might lack free
will. Perhaps, however, this defect in Frankfurt's account can
be remedied by bring in the Second Reason in favour of free will
and requiring that a person's second-order volitions must be his
or her *choice*.

But even if second-order desires are not the whole of free
will, they and in particular second-order volitions are an important part of it. We would not attribute free will to a 'wanton'.

fourth reason: powers of reasoning
We have powers of reasoning. We not only act for reasons, we
can evaluate these reasons retrospectively to see whether they
were good reasons. Hence we have free will.

Reason is essential to free will; a being without powers of
reason could not have free will. Free will might even be defined
as the ability to will in accordance with one's reason whichever
way it inclines one. We have the ability to will (or choose)
otherwise than we do in the sense that if we considered the
reasons for doing otherwise to be better than the reasons for
acting as we do, we would, other things being equal, will (or
choose) differently.

One of the important features of reason is the way that it
allows us to 'transcend' determinism. We are not locked into
a circle of cause and effect, i.e. always doing the same thing in
the same circumstances. We can reflect on whether this is the
best thing to do in the circumstances and decide to do something else instead. We can learn from experience through

thinking about it. Of course, if determinism applies, this process of learning is itself a deterministic process; we can never
'escape' from determinism in a deterministic world. We cannot
literally transcend determinism. But by reflecting on processes
of cause and effect, we can avoid the effects we don't want.
(This is the truth in the Marxist dictum, derived from Hegel, that
freedom is the recognition of necessity.)

Aquinas, influenced by Aristotle, argued for a close connection between free will and practical reasoning, i.e. reasoning
about what to do. Aristotle represented the structure of practical reasoning as a pyramid. At the top is the 'supreme' good
and ultimate end (or goal) which he called 'Eudaimonia' (happiness). At the bottom are all the particular actions which we
choose to perform in our daily lives. Between the top and the
bottom is a complicated structure of means and ends. Particular actions are means to ends which are themselves in turn
means to ends and so on and so forth up to the supreme end
which is not a means to anything further. Since there are many
ways of attaining the end of happiness, we are free to choose
between them according to our understanding and evaluation
of the different possibilities.

We may find that some of our goals conflict. In that case
we must alter our goals, or perhaps we may find that the conflict
is not a real one, or perhaps we can eliminate or tolerate the
ill-effects of the conflict. Because any of our desires may be
opposed to our happiness, all desires are subject to rational
appraisal and one may decide that some desires are bad and
not to be acted on. Since our wills are not *limited* (the only
thing we necessarily desire is the supreme end, and that is not
a *limitation* on the will) – the options are infinite, or practically
infinite, and rational beings like ourselves can choose whichever
option we prefer –, Aquinas believed that we have free will: 'It
is because human beings are rational that their will is necessarily free.'

review of the reasons in favour of free will
It takes only one effective Reason to negate free will, but it takes
more than one to affirm it. The positive case for free will does

not rest on any one Reason, nor have we discussed all the Reasons that have been or might be proposed. Rather, the case for free will depends on all the different facets of human nature and human potentiality which manifest themselves in our thoughts and deeds. The case for free will is cumulative and has many aspects. This allows the possibility of a progressive development of free will both in the history of the species and in the history of the individual, and probably makes it impossible to draw a hard and fast line between creatures with free will and creatures without, or between one's infant self without free will and oneself with.

It may be that the belief in free will is an illusion for the Reasons discussed in chapters 3 to 5. But if those Reasons have not succeeded in refuting free will, then the Reasons we have discussed in this chapter provide some positive considerations in favour of it.

By way of summary, we may say that free will consists in powers of choosing and reasoning and self-reflection, and in the absence of factors which impair or interfere with our powers of decision-making. Our consciousness of being free is important as well, since, as D.C. Dennett observes, 'an agent who enjoyed the other necessary conditions for free will – rationality, and the capacity for higher order self-control and self-reflection – but who had been hoodwinked into believing he lacked free will would be almost as incapacitated for free, responsible choice by that belief as by the lack of any of the other necessary conditions.'

There is one important argument for free will which we have not yet looked at, and that is the argument that we have free will because we are morally responsible: moral responsibility implies free will. This topic is important enough to deserve a chapter on its own.

notes

First Reason
Hobbes, Kant, Spinoza. See ch. 2.

Skinner's Walden Two. See ch. 1.

Henry Sidgwick, 19th century English moral philosopher. The quotation is from his *Methods of Ethics* (1877), Bk. I, ch. 5.

John Stuart Mill. See ch. 5. The quotation is from the chapter 'The Freedom of the Will' in his *Examination of Sir William Hamilton's Philosophy*, Vol. II.

C.A. Campbell. See ch. 4. The quotations are from 'Is "Freewill" a Pseudo-Problem?' sec. VI, and *Scepticism and Construction*, pp. 131, 135.

Moritz Schlick. See ch. 5. The quotation is from 'When Is a Man Responsible?', sec. 6.

Dr. Samuel Johnson, prominent figure in 18th century English life and letters. The quotations are from Boswell's *Life of Johnson*, 10 October 1769, and 15 April 1778.

Second Reason
Harry Frankfurt, contemporary American philosopher. The quotation is from his article 'Alternate Possibilities and Moral Responsibility', sec. IV.

John Locke. See ch. 2. The quotation is from his *Essay Concerning Human Understanding*, Bk. II, ch. 21, sec. 10.

Third Reason
Harry Frankfurt (see above). The quotations are from his article 'Freedom of the Will and the Concept of a Person', introduction and secs. II and III. See Gary Watson, 'Free Agency' for a discussion of Frankfurt.

Fourth Reason
G.F. Hegel, 19th century German philosopher. The dictum 'freedom is the recognition of necessity' is discussed in F. Engels, *Anti-Dühring*, ch. 11.

Aquinas. See chs. 2 and 3.

Aristotle. See ch. 2.

Review
D.C. Dennett. See ch. 5. The quotation is from his *Elbow Room*, p. 168.

7: free will and responsibility

This book is about free will, not about responsibility. And a full discussion of responsibility would require another book. But free will and responsibility are so often linked together (and I haven't been able to stop the word 'responsibility' from creeping into our discussions) that we must consider whether, and if so, in what sense, moral responsibility implies free will.

the traditional view

The traditional view is that only those who have free will can be held morally responsible for what they do. Accordingly, if we are morally responsible, we have free will. This traditional view is held not only by those who think we have free will but also by those who think we do not. Some holders of the traditional view assert both our moral responsibility and our free will. Others believe that because we do not have free will we cannot be held morally responsible for our actions.

In this chapter I shall discuss the views of two philosophers who accept the traditional view, M. Schlick and C.A. Campbell; and then I shall look at P.F. Strawson's views on moral responsibility, which suggest that the question of moral responsibility is to some extent independent of the question of free will.

Schlick and Campbell

Schlick and Campbell both think that we are free and responsible for our actions. But their views are very different. Schlick wants to combine responsibility and determinism, while

Campbell believes that responsibility requires 'contra-causal' freedom, i.e. exemption from determinism. (In the terminology employed in ch. 4, Schlick is a Soft Determinist and Campbell is a Libertarian.) Campbell summarises his view as follows:

> If we ask ourselves whether a certain person is morally responsible for a given act (or it may be just 'in general'), what we are considering, it would be said, is whether or not that person is a fit subject upon whom to pass judgement; whether he can fittingly be deemed morally good or bad, morally praiseworthy or blameworthy...The moral 'ought' implies 'can'. If we say that *A* morally ought to have done *X*, we imply that in our opinion, he could have done *X*. But we assign moral blame to a man only for failing to do what we think he morally ought to have done. Hence if we morally blame *A* for not having done *X*, we imply that he could have done *X* even though in fact he did not. In other words, we imply that *A* could have acted otherwise than he did. And that means that we imply, as a necessary condition of a man's being morally blameworthy, that he enjoyed a freedom of a kind not compatible with unbroken causal continuity.

Hence moral responsibility implies 'contra-causal' freedom.

Schlick disagrees. In his view, the only freedom implied by responsibility is freedom from compulsion (and other factors) which hinder a person 'in the realization of his natural desires'. To be responsible for an act (or omission) is, Schlick claims, to be the person whose motives would have had to be influenced in order to prevent the act (or elicit it): 'the "doer" is the one *upon whom the motive must have acted* in order, with certainty, to have prevented the act (or called it forth, as the case may be)':

> The question of who is responsible is the question concerning the *correct point of application of the motive*...We do not charge an insane person with responsibility, for the very reason that he offers no unified point for the application of a motive. It would be pointless to try to affect him by means of promises or threats, when his confused soul fails to respond to such influence because its normal mechanism is out of order...When a man is forced by threats to commit certain acts we do not blame him, but the one who held the pistol at his breast. The reason is clear: the act would have been prevented had we been able to restrain the person who threatened him; and this person is the

one whom we must influence in order to prevent similar acts in the future.

Thus, in the case of a wrongful act, someone is responsible for that act if, and only if, influencing his or her motives would have averted the act. 'Hence the question regarding responsibility is the question: Who, in a given case, is to be punished?'

Schlick is quite right to say that responsibility in his sense does not imply 'contra-causal' freedom. But the reason for this is that responsibility in Schlick's sense does not imply free will at all. Even those who deny that we have free will hold that we are 'responsible' in Schlick's sense. For instance, John Hospers distinguishes 'two levels of moral discourse':

> one (let's call it the upper level) is that of actions; the other (the lower, or deeper, level) is that of the springs of action.

Hospers holds that we do not have free will on the lower, deeper, level but says that it is perfectly correct to hold (some) people responsible on the upper level: 'we are practical beings interested in changing the course of human behaviour'. Hence we designate as responsible on the upper level those whose behaviour we hope to influence, or think we could have influenced, although they are not responsible on the deeper level.

Again, B.F. Skinner holds that we do not have free will, but he would agree that people are responsible in Schlick's sense, since he believes that people's behaviour can be influenced to prevent them doing what we don't want them to do, or, more accurately, to get them to do what we want them to do. In Skinner's opinion the real issue in responsibility is 'controllability'.

Even if people do not have free will, their behaviour is certainly 'controllable': we can avert, or could have averted, unwanted behaviour by techniques of 'behaviour modification'. Those whose behaviour cannot be so modified are to be considered 'non-responsible'. Hence Schlick's discussion of moral responsibility does not prove anything about free will.

Campbell objects to Schlick's interpretation of 'moral responsibility'. He raises several objections, of which this is the first:

> We do not ordinarily consider the lower animals to be morally responsible. But *ought* we not to do so if Schlick is right about what we mean by moral responsibility? It is quite possible, by punishing the dog who absconds with the succulent chops designed for its master's luncheon, favourably to influence its motives in respect of its future behaviour in like circumstances. If moral responsibility is to be linked with punishment as Schlick links it, and punishment conceived as a form of education, we should surely hold the dog morally responsible? The plain fact, of course, is that we don't. We don't, because we suppose that the dog 'couldn't help it': that its action (unlike what we usually believe to be true of human beings) was simply a link in a continuous chain of causes and effects. In other words, we do commonly demand the contra-causal sort of freedom as a condition of moral responsibility.

This argument may be effective against Schlick (though he might be prepared to 'outsmart' Campbell by holding his dog morally responsible). However, it hardly proves Campbell's view. Does anyone (apart from Campbell) believe that the reason why dogs are not morally responsible is that their behaviour is 'simply a link in a continuous chain of causes and effects'? Dogs have no sense of moral right and wrong; so we cannot hold them morally responsible. But it must be remembered that Campbell regards the sense of moral duty as operating outside the 'chain of causes and effects' (see chapter 6, First Reason). Campbell holds that 'contra-causal' freedom manifests itself only when someone follows the sense of duty in opposition to his 'desiring nature'. A dog presumably always follows his desiring nature, hence is not morally responsible.

Campbell has been interpreted as saying that we are morally responsible only for what we do 'contra-causally'. Thus Jonathan Glover writes:

> Campbell says that libertarians need only claim 'contra-causal' freedom for the few cases where strongest desire clashes with duty. But one might feel that rape could normally be causally explained in terms of strongest desires defeating duty, and this explanation would not itself, as Campbell seems to suggest, automatically absolve a man from moral responsibility.

I think this is a misunderstanding. What Campbell is saying is that all of us who are morally responsible, including the rapist so long as he is not (e.g.) insane, *can* act against our strongest desires, but that in order to do so we must employ our 'contra-causal' freedom. Since we *can* act against our strongest desires we are morally responsible, even if we do not in fact act 'contra-causally'.

But does moral responsibility imply the ability to act 'contra-causally'? Campbell thinks it does because of the principle that 'The moral "ought" implies "can" ' (see the first quotation in this section). Let us consider a particular example: a motorist driving carefully and being in no way drunk or impaired runs over a child who darts out into the street from behind a parked car. We say that the driver is not to blame because he 'couldn't help it'. Obviously we do not mean by this that the driver's actions were causally determined (though they may have been). What we mean is that it would be quite unreasonable to expect the driver to have avoided hitting the child. It would be asking too much of the normal person to require that he should have done otherwise in this situation. So the sense in which the moral 'ought' implies 'can' is that if we say someone ought (morally speaking) to do something, we mean that he can reasonably be expected to do it. And if we think he cannot reasonably be expected to do something, then we do not say he ought to do it and do not blame him for not doing it.

Now, when we are talking about moral responsibility, the judgement that someone could reasonably be expected to do something is itself a *moral* judgement. It is a judgement about the moral standards which apply to the situation. Campbell may want to argue that morally speaking we cannot reasonably expect someone to have done otherwise *unless* that person possessed 'contra-causal' freedom. But the principle that the moral 'ought' implies 'can' will not by itself show that Campbell is right. He needs a further argument. In the next section I look at an account of moral responsibilty which suggests that such a further argument is unlikely to be forthcoming.

Strawson

Strawson begins his essay 'Freedom and Resentment' by contrasting two views about determinism and moral responsibility. One group, the 'pessimists', hold that if determinism is true 'then the concepts of moral obligation and responsibility really have no application'. The other group, the 'optimists', hold that 'these concepts and practices in no way lose their *raison d'être* if the thesis of determinism is true'. Schlick is obviously an 'optimist'; Campbell is a 'pessimist', though this is perhaps not an appropriate label since he is optimistic about our free will and responsibility. However, he is pessimistic about the effect of determinism on responsibility: poisonous and lethal. (In the terminology employed in chapter 4, the optimists are Compatibilists, the pessimists are Incompatibilists. Both groups accept the traditional view that moral responsibility implies free will.) Strawson's aim is to show that the optimists have

presented a distorted and 'one-eyed' picture of moral responsibility, but that their fundamental thesis, the irrelevance of
determinism to moral responsibility, is correct.

In Strawson's view the pessimist is right to say that moral
responsibility is not simply a matter of influencing people's
behaviour:

> When his opponent, the optimist, undertakes to show that the
> truth of determinism would not shake the foundations of the
> concept of moral responsibility and of the practices of moral
> condemnation and punishment, he typically refers, in a more
> or less elaborated way, to the efficacy of these practices in
> regulating behaviour in socially desirable ways. These practices
> are represented solely as instruments of policy, as methods of
> individual treatment and social control. The pessimist recoils
> from this picture; and in his recoil there is, typically, an element
> of emotional shock. He is apt to say, among much else, that
> the humanity of the offender himself is offended by *this* picture
> of his condemnation and punishment.

The optimist (e.g. Schlick) adopts what Strawson calls an
'objective' attitude:

> To adopt the objective attitude to another human being is to
> see him, perhaps, as an object of social policy; as a subject for
> what, in a wide range of sense, might be called treatment...
> The objective attitude...cannot include the range of reactive
> feelings and attitudes which belong to involvement or part-
> icipation with others in inter-personal human relationships; it
> cannot include resentment, gratitude, forgiveness, anger, or the
> sort of love which two adults can sometimes be said to feel
> reciprocally, for each other.

In Strawson's view the participant (inter-)personal reactive
attitudes in no way depend for their justification on the falsity
of determinism. After discussing whether determinism should
lead to an objective attitude to others, he concludes:

> So my answer has two parts. The first is that we cannot, as we
> are, seriously envisage ourselves adopting a thoroughgoing
> objectivity of attitude to others as a result of theoretical con-
> viction of the truth of determinism; and the second is that when
> we do in fact adopt such an attitude in a particular case, our
> doing so is not the consequence of a theoretical conviction
> which might be expressed as 'Determinism in this case', but is

> a consequence of our abandoning, for different reasons in different cases, the ordinary inter-personal attitudes.

Faced with the question whether it might not be *rational* to give up our ordinary inter-personal attitudes, if determinism is true, Strawson responds:

> To this I shall reply, first, that such a question could seem real only to one who had utterly failed to grasp the purpose of the preceding answer, the fact of our natural human commitment to ordinary inter-personal attitudes. This commitment is part of the general framework of human life...And I shall reply, second, that if we could imagine what we cannot have, viz. a choice in this matter, then we could choose rationally only in the light of an assessment of the gains and losses to human life, its enrichment or impoverishment; and the truth or falsity of a general thesis of determinism would not bear on the rationality of *this* choice.

The same holds true, in Strawson's opinion, of the distinctively moral reactive attitudes, like moral indignation and moral condemnation. The truth or falsity of determinism is irrelevant to these attitudes. Consequently they in no way depend for their justification on the falsity of determinism.

> Inside the general structure or web of human attitudes and feelings of which I have been speaking, there is endless room for modification, redirection, criticism, and justification. But questions of justification are internal to the structure or relate to modifications internal to it. The existence of the general framework of attitudes itself is something we are given with the fact of human society. As a whole, it neither calls for, nor permits, an external 'rational' justification.

Campbell's argument that the moral 'ought' implies 'can' and that 'can' implies 'contra-causal' freedom is an attempt to provide the sort of 'external "rational" justification' which Strawson considers irrelevant.

Strawson maintains that our general framework of reactive attitudes, moral and non-moral, is founded on the nature of human community and inter-personal relationships. John Stuart Mill proposed much the same view when he wrote that 'whoever cultivates a disposition to wrong, places his mind out of sympathy with the rest of his fellow creatures, and if they are aware of his disposition, becomes a natural object of their active dislike': 'In this way he is certain to be made accountable, at least to his fellow-creatures, through the normal action of their natural sentiments.' Mill, like Strawson, therefore rejects the view 'which makes the subjection of human volitions to the law of Causation seem inconsistent with accountability'.

If Mill and Strawson are right about moral responsibility, what bearing does this have on the question of free will? It seems to me that if they are right, then this provides a strong case for saying that the question of moral responsibility is independent of the question of free will, contrary to what the traditional view implies. But are they right?

Our present framework of attitudes concerning moral responsibility distinguishes, as Strawson points out, between those who are morally responsible and those who are not, either in general or in the particular case. Now, suppose that the Reasons against free will do prove that we lack free will. In that case, if the traditional view is correct, then no one is morally responsible. Accordingly we would be unable to make a distinction between those who are morally responsible and those who are not. This would invalidate our present framework of attitudes. What should we do? It seems to me that we could, whether or not we would, choose to retain our present framework. But this means that the question of moral responsibility is independent of the question of free will, contrary to what the traditional view implies. Strawson says that of course we would retain our present framework. But it is not clear to me whether this would lead him to reject the traditional view or simply insist that we have free will ('and there's an end on't').

There is of course some connection between moral responsibility and free will. In ordinary English speech to say that someone acted 'of her own free will' is to say that she was not subject to compulsion, and obviously we do not blame those who are subject to compulsion unless they could and should resist it. It certainly seems plausible to say, as Schlick does, that moral responsibility requires that the agent 'acted freely' in some sense of those ambiguous words; for otherwise why should we be holding him or her responsible?

But it is nonetheless important to keep the issue of moral responsibility separate from the issue of free will. Moral responsibility is a *moral* question, to be answered by inquiring what standards should be set up for finding people responsible; it is an inquiry into the *justice* of holding some responsible and others not. (Philosophers call this type of inquiry 'normative'.) The issue of free will, on the other hand, is a question about the *reality* of human nature: are we so constituted as to have free will or not? (Philosophers call this type of inquiry 'ontological'.) Hence the traditional view that moral responsibility implies free will turns out to be a *moral* judgement: it affirms the injustice of holding responsible those who lack free will. It is putting the cart before the horse to use our ideas of what is just to prove a fact about ourselves, viz. that we have free will. Hence the traditional view provides a poor argument for the existence of free will.

notes

C.A. Campbell. See chs. 4 and 6 (First Reason). The quotations are from his 'Is "Free Will" a Pseudo-Problem?', secs. 3 and 4.

Moritz Schlick. See ch. 5 (Thirteenth Reason). The quotations are from 'When Is a Man Responsible?', sec. 5.

John Hospers. See ch. 5 (Eleventh and Twelfth Reasons). The quotations are from 'What Means This Freedom?', sec. 3.

B.F. Skinner. See chs. 1 and 5 (Eighth Reason). He discusses responsibility in *Beyond Freedom and Dignity*, ch. 4.

Jonathan Glover, contemporary English philosopher. The quotation is from his *Responsibility,* p. 53.

P.F. Strawson, prominent 20th century English philosopher. The quotations are from 'Freedom and Resentment', secs. 1, 4, 6.

J.S. Mill. See ch. 5 (Seventh, Sixteenth Reasons) and 6 (First Reason). The quotation is from 'The Freedom of the Will' in his *Examination of Sir William Hamilton's Philosophy,* vol. II.

For discussion of the moral dimensions of responsibility, see Michael Bavidge's book in this series, *Mad or Bad?*

8: personal postscript

In chapter 1 I suggested that two key features of free will are autonomy and the existence of alternatives. I also said that there are three distinct approaches to the question of free will. In this chapter I present my own conclusions about these topics, not because they are self-evidently correct beyond any possibility of dispute (unfortunately that is not so), but because I think anyone who has read this far deserves to hear the author's own views (but only if he or she wants to!). A philosophy book is like a whodunit. There is more than one possible solution. This is mine — in brief outline because the purpose of this book is to present the different views, not lead up to my own.

I think autonomy is best understood in terms of its literal meaning, 'self rule'. 'Autonomy' means that the plan of one's life is one's own; it is a plan that one has worked out for oneself. To work out a plan is to use one's reason but it doesn't follow at all that one's plan must be totally 'rational' in the sense of not allowing room for spontaneity or play or the emotions or sheer desire.

Alternative possibilities are the alternatives we consider in practical reasoning and between which we choose. Reason can invent new possibilities which have not been previously considered (this is the aspect of our free will which Sartre emphasized). Reason can thus 'transcend' (pass beyond) old possibilities. Our reasoning powers are not limited by any pre-arranged set of alternatives.

I see nothing in the foregoing incompatible with determinism. The sense in which I can choose otherwise than I do, if I have free will, seems quite different from the sense in which I cannot choose otherwise than I do, if determinism is true. In particular, saying that we can choose otherwise than we do is compatible with saying that we would choose otherwise only if there were some different causal factor operating; and saying that we would choose otherwise only if there were some different causal factor operating is compatible with determinism. What actual advantage does non-determinism bring? I know of no account of a non-deterministic free will which could not be 'mimicked' in a deterministic system. Arguments to the contrary, like Descartes' or Sartre's, seem to depend on an under-appreciation of the powers of deterministic systems.

The other Reasons against free will do not seem to me to pose any insuperable objections, though they do show that our freedom is sometimes limited.

Now to the three approaches. In the interim we have learnt that these have names. The first approach (determinism and no free will) is Hard Determinism. The second (free will and no determinism) is Libertarianism. The third approach (determinism compatible with free will) is Compatibilism, of which a species is Soft Determinism (which asserts both determinism and free will). Let me take these in turn.

Hard Determinism. My objection to Hard Determinism is that it fails to make important distinctions. It presents a 'billiard ball' view of human behaviour, as if we were pushed into motion by outside causes just like a billiard ball pushed by another ball. It cannot distinguish between causes which oppress us and limit our free will, on the one hand, and causes which do not, on the other. The only distinctions allowed are between aversive and non-aversive and between conspicuous and inconspicuous causes. But these are not the only important distinctions. A human being seems, according to Hard Determinism, to be in exactly the same position whether her brain is being manipulated by a benevolent scientist or whether she is responding rationally and intelligently to her circumstances. Hard Determinism pays lip-service to human abilities, but it seems in the end to regard human powers of choice and reasoning as illusory.

Libertarianism. This view shares with Hard Determinism the belief that free will is incompatible with determinism. By doing so, it plays into the hands of Hard Determinists, because it is impossible to prove that we are exempt from causality (attempts to do so, based on our consciousness of our free will and on our moral responsibility, turned out to be failures). Given a choice between determinism and free will many people would give up free will. Libertarianism's positive view is also open to objection. Some Libertarians, e.g. Descartes and Chisholm, think that our active selves operate in the world free from causality. Others, e.g. Kant, think that nature is entirely deterministic, so that the self which is exempt from determinism must somehow be 'outside' the world. Both alternatives lead to a dualism of 'selves' and other things. Those (I include myself) who believe in a continuity in nature between the lowest animals and ourselves reject both alternatives.

Soft Determinism. Soft Determinists have often presented crude and oversimplified views of human psychology indistinguishable from those of Hard Determinists. Human action is depicted as the outcome of interaction between desires of different strengths, as physical motion is the outcome of interaction between forces of different magnitudes. This way of understanding human behaviour, 'psychological determinism' as it is called, came to the fore in the 17th and 18th centuries in the writings of those influenced by the 'new' mechanical science, especially Hobbes and Hume. On the model of psychological determinism reason ceases to be a controlling force: 'Reason is and ought to be the slave of the passions,' Hume said. This makes it difficult to give a clear sense to the idea that our wills are free. In fact traditional Soft Determinists characteristically *denied* free will. They insisted that the only freedom is freedom to do what one wants. But this is freedom of action, not freedom of will. Someone can have the former but not the latter if she is unable to will or choose otherwise than she does but able to do what she chooses.

If we reject Hard Determinism, Libertarianism and traditional Soft Determinism, we are left only with Compatibilism.

Compatibilism must be distinguished from Soft Determinism, as Anthony Kenny points out:

> Sometimes compatibilism is identified with a philosophical theory which has been nicknamed 'soft determinism': but in reality the two positions are distinct. Soft determinism is a version of determinism: the soft determinist does believe that every event has a cause in the sense of a sufficient antecedent condition. He is called 'soft' because he believes in addition that determinism does not exclude freedom: he is contrasted with the hard determinist who thinks that determinism is incompatible with freedom and that since determinism is true freedom must be an illusion. All soft determinists are compatibilists, but the converse is not true.

Kenny himself rejects psychological determinism, but thinks that physiological determinism might be true. That is to say, he thinks that it might be the case that 'all human activity is determined via neurophysiological states of the brain and central nervous system'. Physiological determinism does not entail psychological determinism. We can affirm the former without affirming the latter:

> Physiological determinism would entail psychological determinism only if physiological events of a particular kind were correlated in a regular and law-like manner with psychological conditions of a particular kind. But there is no reason to believe that physiological determinism must involve such regular correlations. It may be, for all we know, that for each individual case in which a human being can choose whether to do X or not to do X there is a difference between the state of the brain and of the central nervous system which goes with wanting to do X, and the state which goes with not wanting to do X; and this could well be the case without there being any general laws linking physiological states of a particular kind with psychological states of a particular kind. If this is so, there is no reason why physiological determinism should lead to psychological determinism, or why predictability at a physiological level should involve predictability at a psychological level.

Physiological determinism would imply psychological determinism only if there were laws relating (or a 'law-like' relation between) the physiological level and the psychological level.

There might conceivably be such a relationship; but there certainly need not be.

Kenny believes that physiological determinism (whether or not it actually obtains) is compatible with free will. I agree. And I think it is important to emphasize that a justifiable disenchantment with traditional Soft Determinism and psychological determinism need not lead those who believe in free will into the embraces of Libertarianism.

However, if we give up psychological determinism, we must also give up the prospect of *demonstrating* the co-existence of free will and determinism in the way favoured by traditional Soft Determinists. They thought they could demonstrate the existence of free will by providing a deterministic story about people's psychology and then saying, 'Look, there you are, you're free!' They thought they could reconcile our freedom to do otherwise and the necessity of doing what we do by showing that our actual wants and beliefs necessarily lead to one choice and action, whereas if we had other wants and beliefs, they would necessarily lead to other choices and actions. But if psychological determinism is false, the prospect of such demonstrations fades away.

Describing people in terms of physiological determinism is quite different from describing them in psychological terms. And free will is a psychological fact about us. The moral of this is that Compatibilists should not be saddled with the requirement of combining free will and determinism into a single neat picture of human psychology.

Nevertheless, we have very good reasons for believing that we have free will. Even if from the physiologist's standpoint we are deterministic mechanisms, that does not preclude our also being rational, choosing, self-reflective, free-willed creatures.

notes

Hobbes and Hume. See ch. 2. For Hobbes's 'mechanical' view of human psychology see his *Leviathan*. The quotation from Hume is from his *Treatise on Human Nature,* Bk. III, Pt. 1, sec. 1.

Anthony Kenny, contemporary English philosopher. The quotations are from his *Freewill and Responsibility,* pp. 25, 32-3.

suggestions for further reading

The next step for anyone who wants to read further is to look at some of the philosophers we've been discussing. The best way to do this is to consult one or more of the published anthologies of writings on free will. The most recent is Gary Watson, ed., *Free Will.* This is an excellent collection, with a first-rate introduction, and all the articles are worth reading, but it contains nothing pre-1945. The best collection of classic writings on free will is probably Bernard Berofsky, ed., *Free Will and Determinism.* In fact it is hard to imagine a better way of sampling the different approaches to the free will problem than to read the essays reprinted in Berofsky by Schlick, Hobart, Campbell, and Hospers (in that, chronological, order). Another excellent collection, which includes more of the older (18th century and earlier) writers than other collections and also some good 20th century material, is Herbert Morris, ed., *Freedom and Responsibility.* Two other good collections, containing both older and newer writers, are Gerald Dworkin, ed., *Determinism, Free Will, and Moral Responsibility*, and Sidney Morgenbesser and James Walsh, eds., *Free Will.* An interesting collection of papers presented at a conference in New York in 1957 is Sidney Hook, ed., *Determinism and Freedom in the Age of Modern Science.* An excellent anthology of writings on human nature, from ancient Greece to the present, many of which discuss free will, is Leslie Stevenson, ed., *The Study of Human Nature.* For those ready for more difficult reading, John M. Fischer, ed., *Moral Responsibility* (which has a very good introduction) and Ted Honderich, ed., *Essays on*

Freedom of Action both contain some excellent articles. Gary Watson's article 'Free Action and Free Will' provides an up to date survey of writings on free will.

For references to representative writings by Hard Determinists, Libertarians, and Soft Determinists, see the Notes to chapter four and the Bibliography, which contains publication details of the works mentioned here. Two contemporary Compatibilist accounts of free will are Daniel C. Dennett *Elbow Room* and Anthony Kenny *Free will and responsibility*, esp. ch. 2. Responsibility is discussed from a Soft Determinist standpoint in Jonathan Glover *Responsibility*.

For other readings consult the Notes and the Bibliography. Most of the classic philosophers are readily available in paperback editions.

bibliography of 20th century works

___

1. anthologies

Berofsky, Bernard, ed., *Free Will and Determinism* (New York and London, Harper & Row, 1966).

Dworkin, Gerald, ed., *Determinism, Free Will, and Moral Responsibility* (Englewood Cliffs, N.J., and London, Prentice-Hall, 1970).

Fischer, John Martin, ed., *Moral Responsibility* (Ithaca, N.Y., and London, Cornell University Press, 1986).

Honderich, Ted, ed., *Essays on Freedom of Action* (London, Routledge & Kegan Paul, 1973).

Hook, Sidney, ed., *Determinism and Freedom in the Age of Modern Science* (New York, Collier, 1961).

Morgenbesser, Sidney, and James Walsh, eds., *Free Will* (Englewood Cliffs, N.J., and London, Prentice-Hall, 1962).

Morris, Herbert, ed., *Freedom and Responsibility* (Stanford, Stanford University Press, 1961).

Stevenson, Leslie, ed., *The Study of Human Nature* (New York and Oxford, Oxford University Press, 1981).

Watson, Gary, ed., *Free Will* (Oxford, Oxford University Press, 1982).

2. books and articles

The anthologies listed above are referred to below solely by the editors' names (* indicates that only part of a work is reprinted).

Ayer, A.J., 'Fatalism', in *The Concept of a Person* (London, Macmillan, 1973).

Ayer, A.J., 'Freedom and Necessity', in *Philosophical Essays* (London, Macmillan, 1954). In Watson.

Bavidge, Michael, *Mad or Bad?* (Bristol, Bristol Classical Press, 1989).

Berlin, Isaiah, *Historical Inevitability* (Oxford, Oxford University Press, 1954). Reprinted in *Four Essays on Liberty* (Oxford, Oxford University Press, 1969).

Bridgman, Percy W., 'Determinism in Modern Science'. In Hook.

Brown, Geoffrey, *Minds, Brains and Machines* (Bristol, Bristol Classical Press, 1989).

Campbell, C.A., 'Is "Freewill" a Pseudo-Problem?', *Mind* (1951). In Berofsky*; in Morris.

Chisholm, Roderick., 'Responsibility and Avoidability'. In Hook.

Copi, Irving M., *Introduction to Logic* (New York, Macmillan; London, Collier Macmillan, 1986 (7th ed.)).

Dawkins, Richard, *The Selfish Gene* (Oxford, Oxford University Press, 1976).

Dennett, Daniel C., *Elbow Room* (Cambridge, Mass. and London, MIT Press, 1984).

Edwards, Paul, 'Hard and Soft Determinism'. In Hook.

Feinberg, Joel, 'Psychological Egoism'. In Joel Feinberg, ed., *Reason and Responsibility* (California, Wadsworth, 1985 (6th ed.)).

Frankfurt, Harry, 'Alternate Possibilities and Moral Responsibility', *Journal of Philosophy* (1969). In Fischer.

Frankfurt, Harry, 'Freedom of the Will and the Concept of a Person', *Journal of Philosophy* (1971). In Fischer; in Watson.

Glover, Jonathan, *Responsibility* (London, Routledge & Kegan Paul, 1970).

Greenspan, Patricia, 'Behaviour Control and Freedom of Action', *Philosophical Review* (1978). In Fischer.

Hobart, R.E., 'Free Will as Involving Determination and Inconceivable Without It', *Mind* (1934). In Berofsky.

Hook, Sidney. 'Necessity, Indeterminism, and Sentimentalism'. In Hook; in Berofsky*.

Hospers, John, 'Free Will and Psychoanalysis'. (Originally published as 'Meaning and Free Will', *Philosophy and Phenomenological Research* [1950]). In Morris*.

Hospers, John, 'What Means This Freedom?' In Hook; in Berofsky.

Huxley, Aldous, *Brave New World* (New York, Harper & Row, 1946).

Kenny, Anthony, *Freewill and Responsibility* (London, Routledge & Kegan Paul, 1978).

Lorenz, Konrad, *On Aggression* (London, Methuen, 1966).

Lorenz, Konrad, 'Part and Parcel in Animal and Human Societies', in *Studies in Animal and Human Behaviour*, Vol. II. (Cambridge, Mass., Harvard University Press, 1971). In Stevenson*.

Midgley, Mary, *Beast and Man* (London, Methuen, 1980).

Midgley, Mary, 'Gene-Juggling', *Philosophy* (1979). Reprinted in Ashley Montagu, ed., *Sociobiology Examined* (New York and Oxford, Oxford University Press, 1980).

Nagel, Thomas, 'Moral Luck', in *Mortal Questions* (Cambridge, Cambridge University Press, 1979). In Watson.

Nowell-Smith, Patrick, 'Free Will and Moral Responsibility', *Mind* (1948).

Ryle, Gilbert, 'It Was To Be', in *Dilemmas* (Cambridge, Cambridge University Press, 1954).

Sartre, Jean-Paul, *Existentialism and Humanism* (London, Methuen, 1958).

Schlick, Moritz, 'When is a Man Responsible?', in *Problems of Ethics,* trans. D. Rynin (New York, Prentice-Hall, 1939). In Berofsky.

Skinner, B.F., *Beyond Freedom and Dignity* (New York, Knopf, 1971).

Skinner, B.F., *Science and Human Behaviour* (New York, Macmillan, 1953). In Stevenson*.

Skinner, B.F., *Walden Two* (New York, Macmillan, 1948).

Strawson, P.F., 'Freedom and Resentment', *Proceedings of the British Academy* (1962). In Watson.

Taylor, Richard, 'Determinism and the Theory of Agency'. In Hook.

Trigg, Roger, *The Shaping of Man* (Oxford, Blackwell, 1982).

Turing, Alan, 'Computing Machinery and Intelligence', *Mind* (1950). Reprinted in A.R. Anderson, ed., *Minds and Machines* (Englewood Cliffs, N.J., Prentice-Hall, 1964).

Watson, Gary, 'Free Agency', *Journal of Philosophy* (1975). In Fischer; in Watson.

Wilson, E.O. *On Human Nature* (Cambridge, Mass., Harvard University Press, 1978). In Stevenson*.

The following list contains advanced material suitable only for those with a good grounding in philosophy.

Austin, J.L., 'Ifs and Cans', *Proceedings of the British Academy* (1956). In Berofsky; in Morris.

Campbell, C.A., *Scepticism and Construction* (London, Allen and Unwin, 1931).

Chisholm, Roderick, 'Human Freedom and the Self'. In Watson.

Chisholm, Roderick., 'J.L. Austin's Philosophical Papers', *Mind* (1964). In Berofsky*.

Davidson, Donald, 'Freedom to Act'. In Honderich.

Dennett, Daniel C., 'Mechanism and Responsibility'. In Honderich; in Watson.

Foot, Philippa, 'Free Will as Involving Determinism', *Philosophical Review* (1957). In Berofsky; in Morgenbesser and Walsh.

Frankfurt, Harry, 'Three Concepts of Free Action', *Aristotelian Society Supplementary Volume* (1975). In Fischer.

Goldman, A.I., 'The Compatibility of Mechanism and Purpose', *Philosophical Review* (1969).

Kenny, Anthony, 'Freedom, Spontaneity and Indifference'. In Honderich.

Kenny, Anthony, *Will, Freedom and Power* (Oxford, Blackwell, 1975).

Locke, Don, 'Three Concepts of Free Action', *Aristotelian Society Supplementary Volume* (1975). In Fischer.

Malcolm, Norman, 'The Conceivability of Mechanism', *Philosophical Review* (1968). In Watson.

Nowell-Smith, Patrick, 'Ifs and Cans', *Theoria* (1960). In Berofsky.

Nozick, Robert, *Philosophical Explanations* (Cambridge, Mass., Harvard University Press, 1981).

Ross, W.D., 'Indeterminacy and Indeterminism', in *Foundations of Ethics* (Oxford, Clarendon Press, 1939). In Morris*.

Sartre, Jean-Paul, *Being and Nothingness,* trans. H. Barnes (London, Methuen, 1957). In Berofsky*; in Morgenbesser and Walsh*; in Morris*; in Stevenson*.

van Inwagen, Peter, *An Essay on Free Will* (Oxford, Oxford University Press, 1983).

van Inwagen, Peter, 'The Incompatibility of Free Will and Determinism', *Philosophical Studies* (1975). In Watson.

Watson, Gary, 'Free Action and Free Will', *Mind* (1987).

page references to anthologies

Many of the passages quoted in this book can be found in one or more of the anthologies listed in Suggestions for Further Reading. (See section 1 of the Bibliography for publication details.)

page	author	references
4	Sartre	Stevenson 279-80
7	Plato	Stevenson 55
9	Aristotle	Morris 20, 19, 24
10	Aquinas	Morgenbesser & Walsh 30-1; Morris 437-8; Stevenson 75-6
10	Aquinas	Morris 439
12	Descartes	Morris 376
13	Spinoza	Stevenson 98-9, 96, 99-100, 101
14-15	Hobbes and Bramhall	Morgenbesser & Walsh 42, 42-3, 44, 42
15-16	Locke	Morris 65, 60, 61
16-17	Hume	Dworkin 15, 25; Morris 442, 446-7; Stevenson 113-14, 117
21	Sartre	Berofsky 177; Morgenbesser & Walsh 97; Morris 137; Stevenson 270
33	Aquinas	Morgenbesser & Walsh 29; Morris 55
52-3	Nowell-Smith and Campbell	Berofsky 121; Morris 480
64	Eddington and Hobart	Berofsky 81-2
68-9	Hobart	Berofsky 81
69-70	Augustine	Berofsky 272, 275, 276-7
71	Descartes	Stevenson 84

glossary

a priori: a statement is true *a priori* if it can be known to be true independently of experience and observation, by the use of one's reason alone. Mathematical truths are usually considered *a priori*.

argument: an argument is a set of propositions or statements which purport to prove that a certain proposition or statement (the conclusion) is true.

Cartesian: as held or proposed by the philosopher Descartes. Cartesian dualism is the view that human beings are composed of a non-physical mind and a physical body; the mind is the person's 'self' and can survive the death of the body.

categorical: a categorical statement is an unconditional statement, one which does not contain an 'if' clause.

causation: the process whereby one event brings about another event. (Cf. **determinism**.)

compatibilism: the view that free will is compatible with determinism.

compatible: two things are compatible if they can co-exist; neither excludes the other.

conclusion: the conclusion of an argument is the proposition or statement whose truth the argument attempts to prove.

consistent: two propositions or statements are consistent if they can both be true (though they may not both be true in fact; indeed both may be false).

contingent: a contingent proposition or statement is one that could be true and could be false: it is neither necessarily true nor necessarily false. A contingent truth is one that happens to be true, but could have been false.

contra-causal: involving an exemption from, or not being subject to, causal determinism.

contradiction: see **self-contradictory**.

converse: the converse of a statement is that statement but with subject and predicate terms reversed. Thus the converse of 'All cats are mammals' is 'All mammals are cats'.

deductive: a deductive argument is one whose premises are supposed to entail its conclusion.

determinism: the view that every event is caused by antecedent events in such a way that no other event could be brought about by those antecedent events. (See ch. 3.)

dualism: the view that mind and body are distinct from each other (though on some dualist views, e.g. Descartes', they causally interact with each other); the mind, unlike the body, is not physical and is not governed by physical laws.

egoism, psychological: the view that everyone pursues their own self-interest.

empirical: an empirical statement is one whose truth or falsity can be established only by observation.

empiricism: the view that knowledge depends on observation and that it is impossible to acquire any substantive knowledge on the basis of reason alone. Empiricists tend to regard *a priori* truths as tautologies or as derived from tautologies.

entail: one statement entails another when it is self-contradictory to affirm the first and deny the second.

entity: an existing object.

epistemology: the branch of philosophy which studies knowledge, e.g. when are we justified in claiming to know something?

existentialism: the view that we are free to choose our own nature; we do not have any fixed 'essence', or nature, which determines our choices.

fallacy: an error in reasoning.

fatalism: the view that the future is fixed in advance, so that nothing we do can make any difference. (See ch. 5.)

God: a perfectly good, all-knowing (omniscient), all-powerful (omnipotent) and therefore unique being.

hard determinism: the view that all our choices and actions are determined and consequently we do not have free will.

hypothetical: a hypothetical statement is a conditional statement, i.e. one which contains an 'if' clause.

imply: one statement implies another if the truth of the one is a sufficient condition of the truth of the other.

impossibility: what cannot be. (See **possibility**.)

incompatibilism: the view that free will and determinism are incompatible.

incompatible: two things are incompatible if they cannot co-exist; each excludes the other.

inconsistent: two propositions or statements are inconsistent if they cannot both be true; the truth of one is a sufficient condition of the falsity of the other.

indefinite: vague, lacking a fixed boundary or limit.

indeterminism: the denial of determinism, i.e. at least some events are not completely determined by antecedent events.

induction: the process of reasoning leading from observations to the establishment of an empirical statement.

infinite: not possessing any boundary or limit. The series of natural numbers (1, 2, 3, etc.) is usually considered infinite since it has no end (there is no highest number).

law, scientific: a universally true statement describing the relationship between events in nature.

libertarianism: the view that we have free will and that free will is incompatible with determinism; therefore we possess contra-causal freedom.

logic: the study of argument and reasoning which seeks to distinguish valid from invalid forms of argument.

materialism: the view that everything which exists is material, i.e. consists of matter.

metaphysics: the branch of philosophy which is concerned with the nature of reality, e.g. is materialism true?

naturalism: the view that human beings are part of nature and that there is no radical discontinuity between us and lower animals. (Note: the term 'naturalism' also has other meanings.)

necessary condition: a condition that must be fulfilled in order for a given thing to exist or a given statement to be true. *A* is a necessary condition of *B* when the non-existence (or falsity) of *A* implies the non-existence (or falsity) of *B*.

necessary consequence: one statement is a necessary consequence of another when it is impossible for the latter to be true and the former false; if *A* is a necessary consequence of *B* then the truth of *B* is a sufficient condition of the truth of *A*.

necessary truth: one that cannot be false, must be true.

necessity: what must be. There are different kinds of necessity, for example (1) logical necessity, e.g. it is a logical necessity that the conclusion of a sound deductive argument is true; (2) physical necessity, e.g. it is a physical necessity that physical objects behave in the way that physical laws say they do.

normative: a normative inquiry is one which seeks to establish standards of how things ought to be; such inquiries include but are not limited to moral inquiries.

ontology: the study of existence and reality.

physical: a physical object is one studied by the science of physics; its behaviour cannot contravene scientific (physical) laws.

possibility: what can be. There are different kinds of possibility corresponding to the different kinds of necessity. Logical possibility is what is not ruled out by the laws of logic; physical possibility is what is not ruled out by the laws of physics; etc.

predictability: the possibility that an event can be predicted, e.g. on the basis of scientific laws.

premise: the premises of an argument are the propositions or statements from which the conclusion is drawn. ('Premise' is also spelled 'premiss'.)

proposition: the content of a belief or statement. A proposition has a truth-value and is expressible in a sentence: e.g. the belief that it is raining has as its content the proposition that it is raining, which is true when it is raining, and is expressible in the English sentence 'It is raining'.

rationalism: the view that knowledge depends on the use of reason, and that reason is the source of genuine, substantive knowledge.

self-contradictory: a statement is self-contradictory if it contains the denial of its own truth, e.g. 'Circles are square', or if it asserts inconsistent propositions, e.g. 'All men are mortal, but some men are not mortal'.

self-evident: a statement is self-evident if it can be known to be true merely by understanding it, e.g. 'Circles are round'.

soft determinism: the view that all our choices and actions are determined but that we nevertheless have free will.

sound: a sound deductive argument is one which is valid and has true premises.

statement: a proposition claimed to be true, or whose truth is being examined.

substance: an object capable of existing on its own independently of other substances.

sufficient condition: the truth of one statement is a sufficient condition of the truth of another if the latter is a necessary consequence of the former.

tautology: a statement which repeats itself, e.g. 'A triangle is a triangle', or which asserts nothing, e.g. 'Either it's raining or it's not raining'.

teleological: having to do with purposes. A teleological explanation of an action explains it in terms of its purpose.

truth-value: the truth-values are 'true' and 'false'; to have a truth-value is to be either true or false.

valid: a valid deductive argument is one whose premises entail its conclusion.

volition: an act of willing.

index of names